# THE MASTERY OF
# LOVE

*Also by don Miguel Ruiz*

THE FOUR AGREEMENTS
A Practical Guide to Personal Freedom

THE FOUR AGREEMENTS COMPANION BOOK
Using the Four Agreements to Master
the Dream of Your Life

THE FOUR AGREEMENTS AUDIO
Read by actor Peter Coyote

PRAYERS
A Communion with our Creator

LOS CUATRO ACUERDOS
Una guía practica para la libertad personal

CUADERNO DE TRABAJO DE LOS CUATRO ACUERDOS
Utiliza los Cuatro Acuerdos para gobernar
el sueño de tu vida

LA MAESTRÍA DEL AMOR
Una guía practica para el arte de las relaciones

ORACIONES
Una comunión con nuestro Creador

A Practical Guide to the Art of Relationship

A

Toltec

# THE MASTERY OF
# LOVE

Wisdom

Book

DON MIGUEL RUIZ

AMBER-ALLEN PUBLISHING
SAN RAFAEL, CALIFORNIA

Copyright © 1999 by Miguel Angel Ruiz, M.D.

Published by Amber-Allen Publishing, Inc.
Post Office Box 6657
San Rafael, California 94903

Editorial: Janet Mills
Jacket Illustration: Nicholas Wilton, Studio Zocolo
Jacket Design: Michele Wetherbee
Typography: Rick Gordon, Emerald Valley Graphics
Author Photograph: Ellen Denuto

**Library of Congress Cataloging-in-Publication Data**
Ruiz, Miguel, 1952–  The mastery of love : a practical guide to the art
of relationship / Miguel Ruiz.  p. cm. — (A Toltec wisdom book)
ISBN 1-878424-44-0 (alk. paper)
I. Love — Religious aspects — Miscellanea.
I. Title.   II. Series: Ruiz, Miguel, 1952–   Toltec wisdom book.
BL626.4.R85  1999        99-18199
299'.792 — dc21      CIP

Printed in Canada
Distributed by Publishers Group West

10   9   8   7   6   5   4   3   2

To my parents, my children, my siblings,
and the rest of my family,
with whom I am bonded not only by love,
but by our blood and ancestral roots.

To my spiritual family,
with whom I am bonded by our decision
to create a family based on unconditional love,
mutual respect, and the practice
of the Mastery of Love.

And to my human family,
whose minds are fertile for the seeds
of love contained in this book.
May these seeds of love flourish in your life.

# Contents

# CONTENTS

## Note

To avoid using the masculine gender exclusively when referring to both male and female readers, we have randomly used masculine and feminine pronouns throughout the book.

# Acknowledgments

I WISH TO EXPRESS MY GRATITUDE TO JANET MILLS who, like a mother with her own child, gave form to this book with all her love and dedication.

I would also like to thank those people who gave of their time and their love, and helped us with the realization of this book.

Finally, I want to express my gratitude to our Creator for the inspiration and beauty that gave this book Life.

A Toltec is an artist of Love,
an artist of the Spirit,
someone who is creating every moment,
every second, the most beautiful art —
the Art of Dreaming.

Life is nothing but a dream,
and if we are artists,
then we can create our life with Love,
and our dream becomes
a masterpiece of art.

# The Toltec

THOUSANDS OF YEARS AGO, THE TOLTEC WERE known throughout southern Mexico as "women and men of knowledge." Anthropologists have spoken of the Toltec as a nation or a race, but, in fact, the Toltec were scientists and artists who formed a society to explore and conserve the spiritual knowledge and practices of the ancient ones. They came together as masters *(naguals)* and students at Teotihuacan, the ancient city of pyramids outside Mexico City known as the place where "Man Becomes God."

Over the millennia, the *naguals* were forced to conceal the ancestral wisdom and maintain its existence in obscurity. European conquest, coupled with rampant misuse of personal power by a few of the apprentices, made it necessary to shield the knowledge from those who were not prepared to use it wisely or who might intentionally misuse it for personal gain.

Fortunately, the esoteric Toltec knowledge was embodied and passed on through generations by different lineages of *naguals*. Though it remained veiled in secrecy for hundreds of years, ancient prophecies foretold the coming of an age when it would be necessary to return the wisdom to the people. Now, don Miguel Ruiz, a *nagual* from the Eagle Knight lineage, has been guided to share with us the powerful teachings of the Toltec.

Toltec knowledge arises from the same essential unity of truth as all the sacred esoteric traditions found around the world. Though it is not a religion, it honors all the spiritual masters who have taught on the earth. While it does embrace spirit, it is most accurately described as a way of life, distinguished by the ready accessibility of happiness and love.

## INTRODUCTION

# The Master

The Master lives within everyone. When you give food to the one who is starving, when you give water to the one who is thirsty, when you cover the one who is cold, you give your love to the Master.

## INTRODUCTION

# The Master

ONCE UPON A TIME, A MASTER WAS TALKING TO A crowd of people, and his message was so wonderful that everyone felt touched by his words of love. In the crowd there was a man who had listened to every word the Master said. This man was very humble, and he had a great heart. He was so touched by the Master's words that he felt the need to invite the Master to his home.

When the Master finished speaking, the man walked through the crowd, looked into the eyes of the Master, and told him, "I know you are busy and everyone wants your attention. I know you hardly have time to even listen to my words. But my heart is so open and I feel so much love for you that I have the need to invite you to my home. I want to prepare the best meal for you. I don't expect you will accept, but I just had to let you know."

The Master looked into the man's eyes, and with the most beautiful smile he said, "Prepare everything. I will be there." Then the Master walked away.

At these words, the joy in the man's heart was strong. He could hardly wait to serve the Master and to express his love for him. This would be the most important day of his life: The Master was going to be with him. He bought the best food and wine, and found the most beautiful clothes to offer as a gift to the Master. Then he ran home to prepare everything to receive the Master. He cleaned his entire house, prepared the most wonderful meal, and made the table look beautiful. His heart was full of joy because the Master would soon be there.

The man was waiting anxiously when someone knocked at the door. Eagerly, he opened the door, but instead of the Master, he found an old woman. She looked into his eyes and said, "I am starving. Can you give me a piece of bread?"

The man was a little disappointed because it was not the Master. He looked at the woman and said, "Please, come into my house." He sat her in the place he had prepared for the Master, and gave her the food he had made for the Master. But he was anxious and could hardly wait for her to finish eating. The old woman was touched by the generosity of this man. She thanked him and left.

The man had barely finished preparing the table for the Master again when someone knocked at the door. This time it was another stranger who had traveled across the desert. The stranger looked into the man's face and said, "I am thirsty. Can you give me something to drink?"

The man was a little disappointed again because it was not the Master. He invited the stranger into his home, and sat him in the place he had prepared for the Master. He served the wine he had intended to give the Master. When the stranger left, the man again prepared everything for the Master.

Someone knocked at the door again. When the man opened the door, there stood a child. The child looked up at the man and said, "I am freezing. Can you give me a blanket to cover my body?"

The man was a little disappointed because it was not the Master, but he looked into the eyes of the child and felt love in his heart. Quickly he gathered the clothes he had intended to give the Master, and he covered the child with the clothes. The child thanked him and left.

The man prepared everything again for the Master, and then he waited until it was very late. When he realized the Master was not coming, he was disappointed, but right away he forgave the Master. He said to himself, "I knew I could not expect the Master to come to this humble home. Although he said he would come, something more important must have taken him else-where. The Master did not come, but at least he told me he would, and that is enough for my heart to be happy."

Slowly he put the food away, he put the wine away, and he went to bed. That night he dreamed the Master came to his home. The man was happy to see him, but he didn't know that he was dreaming. "Master you came! You kept your word."

The Master replied, "Yes, I am here, but I was here before. I was hungry, and you fulfilled my need for food. I was thirsty, and you gave me the wine. I was cold, and you covered me with clothes. Whatever you do for others, you do for me."

The man woke up, and his heart was filled with happiness, because he understood what the Master had taught him. The Master loved him so much that he had sent three people to give him the greatest lesson: The Master lives within everyone. When you give food to the one who is starving, when you give water to the one who is thirsty, when you cover the one who is cold, you give your love to the Master.

# 1

## The Wounded Mind

In order to protect our emotional wounds, and because of our fear of being hurt, humans create something very sophisticated in the mind: a big denial system. In that denial system we become the perfect liars. We lie so perfectly that we lie to ourselves and we even *believe* our own lies.

# 1

# The Wounded Mind

PERHAPS YOU HAVE NEVER THOUGHT ABOUT IT, but on one level or another, all of us are masters. We are masters because we have the power to create and to rule our own lives.

Just as societies and religions around the world create incredible mythologies, we create our own. Our personal mythology is populated by heroes and villains, angels and demons, kings and commoners. We create an entire population in our mind, including multiple personalities for ourselves. Then we master the image we are going to use in certain circumstances. We become artists of pretending and projecting our images, and we master whatever we believe we are. When we meet other people, we classify them right away, and assign them a role in our lives. We create an image for others, according to what we believe they are. And we do the same thing with everyone and everything around us.

You have the power to create. Your power is so strong that whatever you believe comes true. You create yourself, whatever you believe you are. You are the way you are because that is what you believe about yourself. Your whole reality, everything you believe, is your creation. You have the same power as any other human in the world. The main difference between you and someone else is how you apply your power, what you create with your power. You may be similar to others in many ways, but no one in the whole world lives her life the way you do.

You have practiced all of your life to be what you are, and you do it so well that you master what you believe you are. You master your own personality, your own beliefs; you master every action, every reaction. You practice for years and years, and you achieve the level of mastery to be what you believe you are. Once we can see that all of us are masters, we can see what kind of mastery we have.

When we are children, and we have a problem with someone, we get angry. For whatever reason, that anger pushes the problem away; we get the result we want. It happens a second time — we react with anger — and now we know if we get angry we push the problem away. Then we practice and practice, until we become masters of anger.

In the same way, we become masters of jealousy, masters of sadness, masters of self-rejection. All of our drama and suffering is by practice. We make an agreement with ourselves, and we practice that agreement until it becomes a whole mastery. The way we think, the way we feel, and the way we act become so routine that we no longer need to put our attention on what we are doing. It is just by action-reaction that we behave a certain way.

To become masters of love, we have to practice love. The art of relationship is also a whole mastery, and the only way to reach mastery is with practice. To master a relationship is therefore about action. It is not about concepts or attaining knowledge. It *is* about action. Of course, to have action, we need to have some knowledge, or at least a little more awareness of the way humans operate.

≈

I want you to imagine that you live on a planet where everyone has a skin disease. For two or three thousand years, the people on your planet have suffered the same disease: Their entire bodies are covered by wounds that are infected, and those wounds really hurt when you touch them. Of course, they believe this is a normal physiology of the skin. Even the medical books describe this disease as a normal condition.

When the people are born, their skin is healthy, but around three or four years of age, the first wounds start to appear. By the time they are teenagers, there are wounds all over their bodies.

Can you imagine how these people are going to treat each other? In order to relate with one another, they have to protect their wounds. They hardly ever touch each other's skin because it is too painful. If by accident you touch someone's skin, it is so painful that right away she gets angry and touches your skin, just to get even. Still, the instinct to love is so strong that you pay a high price to have relationships with others.

Well, imagine that a miracle occurs one day. You awake and your skin is completely healed. There are no wounds anymore, and it doesn't hurt to be touched. Healthy skin you can touch feels wonderful because the skin is made for perception. Can you imagine yourself with healthy skin in a world where everyone has a skin disease? You cannot touch others because it hurts them, and no one touches you because they make the assumption that it will hurt you.

If you can imagine this, perhaps you can understand that someone from another planet who came to visit us would have a similar experience with humans. But it isn't our skin that is full of wounds. What the visitor would discover is that the human mind is sick with a disease called fear. Just like the description of the infected skin, the emotional body is full of wounds, and these wounds are infected with emotional poison. The manifestation of the disease of fear is anger, hate, sadness, envy, and hypocrisy; the result of the disease is all the emotions that make humans suffer.

All humans are mentally sick with the same disease. We can even say that this world is a mental hospital. But this mental disease has been in this world for thousands of years, and the medical books, the psychiatric books, and the psychology books describe the disease as normal. They consider it normal, but I can tell you it is not normal.

When the fear becomes too great, the reasoning mind starts to fail and can no longer take all those wounds with all the poison. In the psychology books we call this a mental illness. We call it schizophrenia, paranoia, psychosis, but these diseases are created when the reasoning mind is so frightened and the wounds so painful, that it becomes better to break contact with the outside world.

Humans live in continuous fear of being hurt, and this creates a big drama wherever we go. The way humans relate to each other is so emotionally painful that for no apparent reason we get angry, jealous, envious, sad. To even say "I love you" can be frightening. But even if it's painful and fearful to have an emotional interaction, still we keep going, we enter into a relationship, we get married, and we have children.

In order to protect our emotional wounds, and because of our fear of being hurt, humans create something very sophisticated in the mind: a big denial system. In that denial system we become the perfect liars. We lie so perfectly that we lie to ourselves and we even *believe* our own lies. We don't notice we are lying, and sometimes even when we know we are lying, we justify the lie and excuse the lie to protect ourselves from the pain of our wounds.

The denial system is like a wall of fog in front of our eyes that blinds us from seeing the truth. We wear a social mask because it's too painful to see ourselves or to let others see us as we really are. And the denial system lets us pretend that everyone believes what we want them to believe about us. We put up these barriers for protection, to keep other people away, but those barriers also keep us inside, restricting our freedom. Humans cover themselves, and protect themselves, and when someone says, "You are pushing my buttons," it is not exactly true. What is true is that you are touching a wound in his mind, and he reacts because it hurts.

When you are aware that everyone around you has emotional wounds with emotional poison, you can easily understand the relationship of humans in what the Toltec call the *dream of hell.* From the Toltec perspective, everything we believe about ourselves, and everything we know about our world, is a dream. If you look at any religious description of *hell*, it is the same as human society, the way we dream. Hell is a place of suffering, a place of fear, a place of war and violence, a place of judgment and no justice, a place of punishment that never ends. There are humans versus humans in a jungle of predators; humans full of judgment, full of blame, full of guilt, full of emotional poison — envy, anger, hate, sadness, suffering. We create all these little demons in our mind because we have learned to dream hell in our own life.

Each of us creates a personal dream for our own self, but the humans before us created a big outside dream, the dream of human society. The outside Dream, or the Dream of the Planet, is the collective Dream of billions of dreamers. The big Dream includes all the rules of society, its laws, its religions, its different cultures, and ways to be. All of this information stored inside our mind is like a thousand voices talking to us at once. The Toltec call this the *mitote*.

The real us is pure love; we are *Life*. The real us has nothing to do with the Dream, but the mitote keeps us from seeing what we really are. When you see the Dream from this perspective, and if you have the awareness of what you are, you see the nonsense behavior of humans, and it becomes amusing. What for everyone else is a big drama, for you becomes a comedy. You can see humans suffering over something that is not important, that is not even real. But we have no choice. We are born in this society, we grow up in this society, and we learn to be like everyone else, playing nonsense all the time, competing with mere nonsense.

Imagine that you could visit a planet where everyone has a different kind of emotional mind. The way they relate to each other is always in happiness, always in love, always in peace. Now imagine that one day you awake on *this* planet, and you no longer have wounds in your emotional body. You are no longer afraid to be who you are. Whatever someone says about you, whatever they do, you don't take it personally, and it doesn't hurt anymore. You no longer need to protect yourself. You are not afraid to love, to share, to open your heart. But no one else is like you. How can you relate with people who are emotionally wounded and sick with fear?

✤

When a human is born, the emotional mind, the emotional body, is completely healthy. Maybe around three or four years of age, the first wounds in the emotional body start to appear and get infected with emotional poison. But if you observe children who are two or three years old, if you see how they behave, they are playing all the time. You see them laughing all the time. Their imagination is so powerful, and the way they dream is an adventure of exploration. When something is wrong they react and defend themselves, but then they just let go and turn their attention to the moment again, to play again, to explore and have fun again. They are living in the moment. They are not ashamed of the past; they are not worried about the future. Little children express what they feel, and they are not afraid to love.

The happiest moments in our lives are when we are playing just like children, when we are singing and dancing, when we are exploring and creating just for fun. It is wonderful when we behave like a child because this is the normal human mind, the normal human tendency. As children, we are innocent and it is natural for us to express love. But what has happened to us? What has happened to the whole world?

What has happened is that when we are children, the adults already have that mental disease, and they are highly contagious. How do they pass this disease to us? They "hook our attention," and they teach us to be like them. That is how we pass our disease to our children, and that is how our parents, our teachers, our older siblings, the whole society of sick people infected us with that disease. They hooked our attention and put information into our mind through repetition. This is the way we learned. This is the way we program a human mind.

The problem is the program, the information we have stored in our mind. By hooking the attention, we teach children a language, how to read, how to behave, how to dream. We domesticate humans the same way we domesticate a dog or any other animal: with punishment and reward. This is perfectly normal. What we call education is nothing but domestication of the human being.

We are afraid to be punished, but later we are also afraid of not getting the reward, of not being good enough for Mom or Dad, sibling or teacher. The need to be accepted is born. Before that, we don't care whether we are accepted or not. People's opinions are not important. They are not important because we just want to play and we live in the present.

The fear of not getting the reward becomes the fear of rejection. The fear of not being good enough for someone else is what makes us try to change, what makes us create an image. Then we try to project that image according to what they want us to be, just to be accepted, just to have the reward. We learn to pretend to be what we are not, and we practice trying to be someone else, just to be good enough for Mom, for Dad, for the teacher, for our religion, for whatever. We practice and practice, and we master how to be what we are not.

Soon we forget who we really are, and we start to live our images. We create not just one image, but many different images according to the different groups of people we associate with. We create an image at home, an image at school, and when we grow up we create even more images.

This is also true for a simple relationship between a man and a woman. The woman has an outer image that she tries to project to others, but when she is alone, she has another image of herself. The man also has an outer image and an inner image. By the time they are adults, the inner image and outer image are so different that they hardly match anymore. In the relationship between a man and woman, there are four images at least. How can they really know each other? They don't. They can only try to understand the image. But there are more images to consider.

When a man meets a woman, he makes an image of her from his point of view, and the woman makes an image of the man from her point of view. Then he tries to make her fit the image he makes for her, and she tries to make him fit the image she makes for him. Now there are six images between them. Of course, they are lying to each other, even if they don't know they are lying. Their relationship is based on fear; it is based on lies. It is not based on truth, because they cannot see through all that fog.

In the period when we are little children, there is no conflict with the images we pretend to be. Our images are not really challenged until we begin to interact with the outside world and no longer have our parents' protection. This is why being a teenager is particularly difficult. Even if we are prepared to support and defend our images, as soon as we try to project our images to the outside world, the world fights back. The outside world starts proving to us, not just privately but publicly, that we are not what we pretend to be.

Let's take the example of a teenage boy who pretends to be very intelligent. He goes to a debate at school, and in that debate someone who is more intelligent and more prepared wins the debate and makes him look ridiculous in front of everyone. He will try to explain and excuse and justify his image in front of his peers. He will be so kind to everyone and will try to save his image in front of them, but he knows he is lying. Of course, he tries his best not to break in front of his peers, but as soon as he is alone and sees himself in a mirror, he goes and breaks the mirror. He hates himself; he feels that he is so stupid, that he is the worst. There is a big discrepancy between the inner image and the image he tries to project to the outside world. The bigger the discrepancy, the more difficult the adaptation to the society Dream, and the less love he will have for himself.

Between the image he pretends to be and the inner image when he is alone are lies and more lies. Both images are completely out of touch with reality; they are false, but he doesn't see that. Maybe someone else can see that, but he is completely blind. His denial system tries to protect the wounds, but the wounds are real, and he is hurting because he is trying so hard to defend an image.

When we are children, we learn that everyone's opinions are important, and we rule our lives according to those opinions. A simple opinion from someone can put us deeper into hell, an opinion that is not even true: "You look ugly. You are wrong. You are stupid." Opinions have a lot of power over the nonsense behavior of people who live in hell. That is why we need to hear that we are good, that we are doing well, that we are beautiful. "How do I look? How was what I said? How am I doing?"

We need to hear the opinions of others because we are domesticated and we can be manipulated by those opinions. That is why we seek recognition from other people; we need emotional support from other people; we need to be accepted by the outside Dream, via other people. That is why teenagers drink alcohol, take drugs, or start smoking. It is just to be accepted by other people who have all those opinions; it is just to be considered "cool."

So many humans are suffering because of all the false images we try to project. Humans pretend to be something very important, but at the same time we believe we are nothing. We work so hard to be some-one in that society Dream, to be recognized and approved by others. We try so hard to be important, to be a winner, to be powerful, to be rich, to be famous, to express our personal dream, and to impose our dream onto other people around us. Why? Because humans believe the Dream is real, and we take it very seriously.

# 2

## The Loss of Innocence

Humans use fear to domesticate humans, and our fear increases with each experience of injustice. The sense of injustice is the knife that opens a wound in our emotional body. Emotional poison is created by our *reaction* to what we consider injustice. Some wounds will heal, others will become infected with more and more poison.

# 2

# The Loss of Innocence

HUMANS BY NATURE ARE VERY SENSITIVE BEINGS. We are so emotional because we perceive everything with the emotional body. The emotional body is like a radio that can be tuned to perceive certain frequencies or to react to certain frequencies. The normal frequency of humans before domestication is to explore and to enjoy life; we are tuned to love. As children, we don't have any definition of love as an abstract concept; we just live love. It's the way we are.

The emotional body has a component like an alarm system to let us know when something is wrong. It is the same with the physical body; it has an alarm system to let us know something is wrong with our body. We call this pain. When we feel pain it is because there is something wrong with the body that we have to look at and fix. The alarm system for the emotional body is fear. When we feel fear, it's because there is something wrong. Perhaps we are in danger of losing our life.

The emotional body perceives emotions, but not through the eyes. We perceive emotions through our emotional body. Children just *feel* emotions and their reasoning mind doesn't interpret or question them. This is why children accept certain people and reject other people. When they don't feel confident around someone, they reject that person because they can feel the emotions that person is projecting. Children can easily perceive when someone is angry and their alarm system generates a little fear that says, "Stay away." And they follow their instinct — they stay away.

We learn to be emotional according to the emotional energy in our home, and our personal reaction to that energy. That is why every brother and sister will react differently according to how they learn to defend themselves and adapt to different circumstances. When our parents are constantly fighting, when there is disharmony, disrespect, and lies, we learn the emotional way of being like them. Even if they tell us not to be that way and not to lie, the emotional energy of our parents, of our entire family, will make us perceive the world in a similar way.

The emotional energy that lives in our home is going to tune our emotional body to that frequency. The emotional body starts to change its tune, and it is no longer the normal tune of the human being. We play the game of the adults, we play the game of the outside Dream, and we lose. We lose our innocence, we lose our freedom, we lose our happiness, and we lose our tendency to love. We are forced to change and we start perceiving another world, another reality: the reality of injustice, the reality of emotional pain, the reality of emotional poison. Welcome to hell — the hell that humans create, which is the Dream of the Planet. We are welcomed into that hell, but we don't invent it personally. It was here before we were born.

You can see how real love and freedom are destroyed by looking at children. Imagine a child two or three years old running and having fun in the park. Mom is there watching the little guy, and she's afraid he might fall and hurt himself. At a certain point she wants to stop him, and the child thinks Mom is playing with him, so he tries to run faster from her. Cars are passing in the street nearby, which makes Mom even more afraid, and finally she catches him. The child is expecting her to play, but she spanks him. Boom! It's a shock. The child's happiness was the expression of love coming out of him and he does not understand why she is acting this way. This is a shock that stops love little by little over time. The child does not understand words, but even so, he can question, "Why?"

Running and playing is an expression of love, but it's no longer safe because your parents punish you when you express your love. They send you to your room, and you cannot do what you want to do. They tell you that you are being a bad boy, or a bad girl, and that puts you down, that means punishment.

In that system of reward and punishment there is a sense of justice and injustice, what is fair and what is not fair. The sense of injustice is like a knife that opens an emotional wound in the mind. Then, according to our reaction to the injustice, the wound may get infected with emotional poison. Why do some wounds get infected? Let's look at another example.

Imagine that you are two or three years old. You are happy, you are playing, you are exploring. You aren't conscious of what is good, what is bad, what is right, what is wrong, what you should be doing, what you shouldn't be doing, because you are not yet domesticated. You are playing in the living room with whatever is around you. You don't have any bad intention, you don't try to hurt anything, but you are playing with your Daddy's guitar. For you, it's just a toy; you don't try to hurt your Daddy at all. But your father is having one of those days when he doesn't feel right. He has problems in his business, and he goes into the living room and finds you playing with his things. He gets mad right away, and he grabs you and spanks you.

This is injustice from your point of view. Your father just comes, and with anger he hurts you. This was someone you trusted completely because he is your Daddy, someone who usually protects you and allows you to play and allows you to be you. Now there is something that doesn't quite fit. That sense of injustice is like a pain in your heart. You feel sensitive; it hurts and makes you cry. But you cry not just because he spanks you. It's not the physical aggression that hurts you; it's the emotional aggression you feel is not fair. *You didn't do anything.*

That sense of injustice opens a wound in your mind. Your emotional body is wounded, and in that moment you lose a little part of your innocence. You learn that you cannot always trust your father. Even if your mind doesn't know that yet, because your mind doesn't analyze, it still understands, "I cannot trust." Your emotional body tells you there is something that you cannot trust, and that something can be repeated.

Your reaction might be fear; your reaction might be anger or being shy or just crying. But that reaction is already emotional poison, because the normal reaction before domestication is that your Daddy spanks you and you want to hit him back. You hit him back, or just intend to put your hand up, and that makes your father even madder at you. The reaction of your father for just putting your hand up against him creates a worse punishment. Now you know he will destroy you. Now you are afraid of him, and you no longer defend yourself because you know it will only make things worse.

You still don't understand why, but you know your father can even kill you. This opens a fierce wound in your mind. Before this, your mind was completely healthy; you were completely innocent. After this, the reasoning mind tries to do something with the experience. You learn to react in a certain way, your personal way. You keep that emotion with you, and it changes your way of life. This experience will repeat itself more often now. The injustice will come from Mom and Dad, from brothers and sisters, from aunts and uncles, from the school, from society, from everyone. With each fear, you learn to defend yourself, but not the way you did before domestication, when you would defend yourself and just keep playing.

Now there is something inside the wound that at first is not a big problem: emotional poison. The emotional poison accumulates, and the mind begins to play with that poison. Now we start to worry a little about the future because we have the memory of the poison and we don't want that to happen again. We also have memories of being accepted; we remember Mom and Dad being good to us and living in harmony. We want the harmony, but we don't know how to create it. And because we are inside the bubble of our own perception, whatever happens around us now seems as if it is *because of us.* We believe Mom and Dad fight because of us, even if it doesn't have anything to do with us.

Little by little we lose our innocence; we start to feel resentment, then we no longer forgive. Over time, these incidents and interactions let us know it's not safe to be who we really are. Of course this will vary in intensity with each human according to his intelligence and his education. It will depend on many things. If you are lucky, the domestication is not that strong. But if you are not so lucky, the domestication can be so strong and the wounds so deep, that you can even be afraid to speak. The result is, "Oh, I am shy." Shyness is the fear of expressing yourself. You may believe you don't know how to dance or how to sing, but this is just repression of the normal human instinct to express love.

⸎

Humans use fear to domesticate humans, and our fear increases with each experience of injustice. The sense of injustice is the knife that opens a wound in our emotional body. Emotional poison is created by our *reaction* to what we consider injustice. Some wounds will heal, others will become infected with more and more poison. Once we are full of emotional poison, we have the need to release it, and we practice releasing the poison by sending it to someone else. How do we do this? By hooking that person's attention.

Let's take an example of an ordinary couple. For whatever reason, the wife is mad. She has a lot of emotional poison from an injustice that comes from her husband. The husband is not home, but she remembers that injustice and the poison is growing inside. When the husband comes home, the first thing she wants to do is hook his attention because once she hooks his attention, all the poison can go to her husband and she can feel the relief. As soon as she tells him how bad he is, how stupid or how unfair he is, that poison she has inside her is transferred to the husband.

She keeps talking and talking until she gets his attention. The husband finally reacts and gets mad, and she feels better. But now the poison is going through him, and he has to get even. He has to hook her attention and release the poison, but it's not just her poison — it's her poison plus his poison. If you look at this interaction, you will see that they are touching each other's wounds and playing ping-pong with emotional poison. The poison keeps growing and growing, until someday one of them is going to explode. This is often how humans relate with each other.

By hooking the attention, the energy goes from one person to another person. The attention is something very powerful in the human mind. Everyone around the world is hunting the attention of others all the time. When we capture the attention, we create channels of communication. The Dream is transferred, power is transferred, but emotional poison is transferred also.

Usually we release the poison with the person we think is responsible for the injustice, but if that person is so powerful that we cannot send it to him, we don't care who we send it to. We send it to the little ones who have no defense against us, and that is how abusive relationships are formed. The people of power abuse the people who have less power because they need to release their emotional poison. We have the need to release the poison, and sometimes we don't want justice; we just want to release, we want peace. That is why humans are hunting power all the time, because the more powerful we are, the easier it is to release the poison to the ones who cannot defend themselves.

Of course, we are talking about relationships in hell. We are talking about the mental disease that exists on this planet. There is no one to blame for this disease; it is not good or bad or right or wrong; it is simply the normal pathology of this disease. No one is guilty for being abusive. Just as people on that imaginary planet are not guilty because their skin is sick, you are not guilty because you have wounds infected with poison. When you are physically sick or injured, you don't blame yourself or feel guilty. Then why feel bad or feel guilty because your emotional body is sick?

What is important is to have the awareness that we have this problem. If we have the awareness, we have the opportunity to heal our emotional body, our emotional mind, and stop the suffering. Without the awareness, there is nothing we can do. The only thing we can do is to keep suffering from the interaction with other humans, but not just with other humans, the interaction with our own self, because we also touch our own wounds just to be punished.

In our mind we create that part of us that is always judging. The Judge is judging everything we do, everything we don't do, everything we feel, everything we don't feel. We are judging ourselves all the time, and we are judging everyone else all the time, based on what we believe and based on the sense of justice and injustice. Of course, we find ourselves guilty and we need to be punished. The other part of our mind that receives the judgment and has the need to be punished is the Victim. That part of us says, "Poor me. I'm not good enough, I'm not strong enough, I'm not intelligent enough. Why should I try?"

When you were a child, you could not choose what to believe and what not to believe. The Judge and the Victim are based on all those false beliefs you didn't choose. When that information went into your mind, you were innocent. You believed everything. The Belief System was put inside you like a program by the outside Dream. The Toltec call this program the *Parasite.* The human mind is sick because it has a Parasite that steals its vital energy and robs it of joy. The Parasite is all those beliefs that make you suffer. Those beliefs are so strong that years later when you learn new concepts and try to make your own decisions, you find those beliefs still control your life.

Sometimes the little child inside you comes out — the real you that stays at the age of two or three years old. You are living in the moment and having fun, but there is something pulling you back; something inside feels unworthy of having too much fun. An inner voice tells you that your happiness is too good to be true; it isn't right to be too happy. All the guilt, all the blame, all the emotional poison in your emotional body keeps pulling you back into the world of drama.

The Parasite spreads like a disease from our grand-parents, to our parents, to ourselves, and then we give it to our own children. We put all those programs inside our children the same way we train a dog. Humans are domesticated animals, and this domestication leads us into the dream of hell where we live in fear. The food for the Parasite is the emotions that come from fear. Before we get the Parasite, we enjoy life, we play, we are happy like little children. But after all that garbage is put into our minds, we are no longer happy. We learn to be right and to make everyone else wrong. The need to be "right" is the result of trying to protect the image we want to project to the outside. We have to impose our way of thinking, not just onto other humans, but even upon ourselves.

With awareness we can easily understand why relationships don't work — with our parents, with our children, with our friends, with our partner, and even with ourselves. Why doesn't the relationship with ourselves work? Because we are wounded and we have all that emotional poison that we can hardly handle. We are full of poison because we grew up with an *image of perfection* that is not true, which does not exist, and in our mind it isn't fair.

We have seen how we create that image of perfection to please other people, even though they create their own dream that has nothing to do with us. We try to please Mom and Dad, we try to please our teacher, our minister, our religion, and God. But the truth is that from their point of view, we are never going to be perfect. That image of perfection tells us how we should be in order to acknowledge that we are good, in order to accept ourselves. But guess what? This is the biggest lie we believe about ourselves, because we are *never* going to be perfect. And there is no way that we can forgive ourselves for not being perfect.

That image of perfection changes the way we dream. We learn to deny ourselves and reject ourselves. We are never good enough, or right enough, or clean enough, or healthy enough, according to all those beliefs we have. There is always *something* the Judge can never accept or forgive. That is why we reject our own humanity; that is why we never deserve to be happy; that is why we are searching for someone who abuses us, someone who will punish us. We have a very high level of self-abuse because of that image of perfection.

When we reject ourselves, and judge ourselves, and find ourselves guilty and punish ourselves so much, it looks like there is no love. It looks like there is only punishment, only suffering, only judgment in this world. Hell has many different levels. Some people are very deep in hell and other people are hardly in hell, but still they are in hell. There are very abusive relationships in hell and relationships with hardly any abuse.

You are no longer a child, and if you have an abusive relationship, it is because you accept that abuse, because you believe you deserve it. You have a limit to the amount of abuse you will accept, but no one in the whole world abuses you more than you abuse yourself. The limit of your self-abuse is the limit you will tolerate from other people. If someone abuses you more than you abuse yourself, you walk away, you run, you escape. But if someone abuses you a little less than you abuse yourself, perhaps you stay longer. You still deserve that abuse.

Usually in a normal relationship in hell, it's about payment for an injustice; it's about getting even. I abuse you the way you need to be abused, and you abuse me the way I need to be abused. We have a good equilibrium; it works. Of course, energy attracts the same kind of energy, the same vibration. If someone comes to you and says, "Oh, I am so abused," and you ask, "Well, why do you stay there?," he doesn't even know why. The truth is he needs that abuse because that is the way he punishes himself.

Life brings to you exactly what you need. There is perfect justice in hell. There is nothing to blame. We can even say that our suffering is a gift. If you just open your eyes and see what is around you, it's exactly what you need to clean your poison, to heal your wounds, to accept yourself, and to get out of hell.

## 3

# The Man Who Didn't
# <u>Believe in Love</u>

What he said was that love is just like a drug; it makes you very high, but it creates a strong need. You can become highly addicted to love, but what happens when you don't receive your daily doses of love? Just like a drug, you need your everyday doses.

# 3

# The Man Who Didn't
Believe in Love

I WANT TO TELL YOU A VERY OLD STORY ABOUT
the man who didn't believe in love. This was an ordinary man just like you and me, but what made this
man special was his way of thinking: He thought *love
doesn't exist.* Of course, he had a lot of experience trying
to find love, and he had observed the people around

him. Much of his life had been spent searching for love, only to find that love didn't exist.

Wherever this man went, he used to tell people that love is nothing but an invention of the poets, an invention of religions just to manipulate the weak mind of humans, to have control over humans, to make them believe. He said that love is not real, and that's why no human could ever find love even though he might look for it.

This man was highly intelligent, and he was very convincing. He read a lot of books, he went to the best universities, and he became a respected scholar. He could stand in any public place, in front of any kind of people, and his logic was very strong. What he said was that love is just like a drug; it makes you very high, but it creates a strong need. You can become highly addicted to love, but what happens when you don't receive your daily doses of love? Just like a drug, you need your everyday doses.

He used to say that most relationships between lovers are just like a relationship between a drug addict and the one who provides the drugs. The one who has the biggest need is like the drug addict; the one who has a little need is like the provider. The one who has the little need is the one who controls the whole relationship. You can see this dynamic so clearly because usually in every relationship there is one who loves the most and the other who doesn't love, who only takes advantage of the one who gives his or her heart. You can see the way they manipulate each other, their actions and reactions, and they are just like the provider and the drug addict.

The drug addict, the one who has the biggest need, lives in constant fear that perhaps he will not be able to get the next dosage of love, or the drug. The drug addict thinks, "What am I going to do if she leaves me?" That fear makes the drug addict very possessive. "That's mine!" The addict becomes jealous and demanding, because the fear of not having the next dosage. The provider can control and manipulate the one who needs the drug by giving more doses, fewer doses, or no doses at all. The one who has the biggest need completely surrenders and will do whatever he can to avoid being abandoned.

The man went on explaining to everyone why love doesn't exist. "What humans call 'love' is nothing but a fear relationship based on control. Where is the respect? Where is the love they claim to have? There is no love. Young couples, in front of the representation of God, in front of their family and friends, make a lot of promises to each other: to live together forever, to love and respect each other, to be there for each other, through the good times and the bad times. They promise to love and honor each other, and make promises and more promises. What is amazing, is that they really believe these promises. But after the marriage — one week later, a month later, a few months later — you can see that none of these promises are kept.

"What you find is a war of control to see who will manipulate whom. Who will be the provider, and who will have the addiction? You find that a few months later, the respect they swear to have for each other is gone. You can see the resentment, the emotional poison, how they hurt each other, little by little, and it grows and grows, until they don't know when the love stops. They stay together because they are afraid to be alone, afraid of the opinions and judgments of others, and also afraid of their own judgments and opinions. But where is the love?"

He used to claim that he saw many old couples that had lived together thirty years, forty years, fifty years, and they were so proud to have lived together all those years. But when they talked about their relationship, what they said was, "We survived the matrimony." That means one of them surrendered to the other; at a certain time, she gave up and decided to endure the suffering. The one with the strongest will and less need won the war, but where is that flame they call love? They treat each other like a possession: "She is mine." "He is mine."

The man went on and on about all the reasons why he believed love doesn't exist, and he told others, "I have done all that already. I will no longer allow anyone to manipulate my mind and control my life in the name of love." His arguments were quite logical, and he convinced many people by all his words. *Love doesn't exist.*

Then one day this man was walking in a park, and there on a bench was a beautiful lady who was crying. When he saw her crying, he felt curiosity. Sitting beside her, he asked if he could help her. He asked why she was crying. You can imagine his surprise when she told him she was crying because love doesn't exist. He said, "This is amazing — a woman who believes that love doesn't exist!" Of course, he wanted to know more about her.

"Why do you say that love doesn't exist?" he asked.

"Well, it's a long story," she replied. "I married when I was very young, with all the love, all these illusions, full of hope that I would share my life with this man. We swore to each other our loyalty, respect, and honor, and we created a family. But soon everything changed. I was the devoted wife who took care of the children and the home. My husband continued to develop his career, and his success and image outside of home was more important to him than our family. He lost respect for me, and I lost respect for him. We hurt each other, and at a certain point I discovered that I didn't love him and he didn't love me either.

"But the children needed a father, and that was my excuse to stay and to do whatever I could to support him. Now the children are grown and they have left. I no longer have any excuse to stay with him. There's no respect, there's no kindness. I know that even if I find someone else, it's going to be the same, because love doesn't exist. There is no sense to look around for something that doesn't exist. That is why I am crying."

Understanding her very well, he embraced her and said, "You are right; love doesn't exist. We look for love, we open our heart and we become vulnerable, just to find selfishness. That hurts us even if we don't think we will be hurt. It doesn't matter how many relationships we have; the same thing happens again and again. Why even search for love any longer?"

They were so much alike, and they became the best friends ever. It was a wonderful relationship.

They respected each other, and they never put each other down. With every step they took together, they were happy. There was no envy or jealousy, there was no control, there was no possessiveness. The relationship kept growing and growing. They loved to be together, because when they were together they had a lot of fun. When they were not together, they missed each other.

One day when the man was out of town, he had the weirdest idea. He was thinking, "Hmm, maybe what I feel for her is love. But this is so different from what I have ever felt before. It's not what the poets say it is, it's not what religion says, because I am not responsible for her. I don't take anything from her; I don't have the need for her to take care of me; I don't need to blame her for my difficulties or to take my dramas to her. We have the best time together; we enjoy each other. I respect the way she thinks, the way she feels. She doesn't embarrass me; she doesn't bother me at all. I don't feel jealous when she's with other people; I don't feel envy when she is successful.

Perhaps love *does* exist, but it's not what everyone thinks love is."

He could hardly wait to go back home and talk to her, to let her know about his weird idea. As soon as he started talking, she said, "I know exactly what you are talking about. I had the same idea long ago, but I didn't want to share it with you because I know you don't believe in love. Perhaps love does exist, but it isn't what we thought it was." They decided to become lovers and to live together, and it was amazing that things didn't change. They still respected each other, they were still supportive of each other, and the love grew more and more. Even the simplest things made their hearts sing with love because they were so happy.

The man's heart was so full with all the love he felt that one night a great miracle happened. He was looking at the stars and he found the most beautiful one, and his love was so big that the star started coming down from the sky and soon that star was in his hands. Then a second miracle happened, and his soul merged with that star. He was intensely happy, and he could hardly wait to go to the woman and put that star in her hands to prove his love to her. As soon as he put the star in her hands, she felt a moment of doubt. This love was overwhelming, and in that moment, the star fell from her hands and broke in a million little pieces.

Now there is an old man walking around the world swearing that love doesn't exist. And there is a beautiful old woman at home waiting for a man, shedding a tear for a paradise that once she had in her hands, but for one moment of doubt, she let it go. This is the story about the man who didn't believe in love.

Who made the mistake? Do you want to guess what went wrong? The mistake was on the man's part in thinking he could give the woman his happiness. The star was his happiness, and his mistake was to put his happiness in her hands. Happiness never comes from outside of us. He was happy because of the love coming out of him; she was happy because of the love coming out of her. But as soon as he made her responsible for his happiness, she broke the star because she could not be responsible for his happiness.

No matter how much the woman loved him, she could never make him happy because she could never know what he had in his mind. She could never know what his expectations were, because she could not know his dreams.

If you take your happiness and put it in someone's hands, sooner or later, she is going to break it. If you give your happiness to someone else, she can always take it away. Then if happiness can only come from inside of you and is the result of your love, you are responsible for your happiness. We can never make anyone responsible for our own happiness, but when we go to the church to get married, the first thing we do is exchange rings. We put our star in each other's hands, expecting that she is going to make you happy, and you are going to make her happy. It doesn't matter how much you love someone, you are never going to be what that person wants you to be.

That is the mistake most of us make right from the beginning. We base our happiness on our partner, and it doesn't work that way. We make all those promises that we cannot keep, and we set ourselves up to fail.

# 4

## The Track of Love,
## The Track of Fear

If you catch yourself in the track of
fear, just by having that awareness,
you can shift your attention into the
track of love. Just by seeing where you
are, just by changing your attention,
everything around you will change.

# 4

# The Track of Love, The Track of Fear

YOUR WHOLE LIFE IS NOTHING BUT A DREAM. YOU live in a fantasy where everything you know about yourself is only true for you. Your truth is not the truth for anyone else, and that includes your own children or your own parents. Just consider what you believe about yourself and what your Mother believes about you. She can say she knows you very well, but she has no idea who you really are. You know that she doesn't. You can believe that you know your Mother very well, but you don't have any idea who she really is. She has all those fantasies in her mind that she never shared with anyone else. You have no idea what is inside her mind.

If you look at your own life and try to remember what you did when you were eleven or twelve years old, you will hardly remember more than 5 percent of your own life. Of course you will remember the most important things, like your own name, because you repeat these all the time. But sometimes you forget the name of your own children or your friends. That's because your life is made by dreams — many little dreams that are changing all the time. Dreams have a tendency to dissolve, and that is why we forget so easily.

Every human being has a personal dream of life, and that dream is completely different from anyone else's dream. We dream according to all the beliefs that we have, and we modify our dream according to the way we judge, according to the way we are victimized. That is why dreams are never the same for any two people. In a relationship, we can pretend to be the same, to think the same, to feel the same, to dream the same, but there is no way that can happen. There are two dreamers with two dreams. Every dreamer is going to dream in his own way. That is why we need to accept the differences that exist between two dreamers; we need to *respect* each other's dream.

We can have thousands of relationships at the same time, but every relationship is between two persons and no more than two. I have a relationship with each one of my friends, and it is just between two.

I have a relationship with each one of my children, and each relationship is completely different from the others. According to the way the two people dream, they create the direction of that dream we call *relationship*. Every relationship we have — with Mom, with Dad, with brothers, with sisters, with friends — is unique because we dream a small dream together.

Every relationship becomes a living being made by two dreamers.

Just as your body is made by cells, your dreams are made by emotions. There are two main sources of those emotions: One is fear, and all the emotions that come from fear; the other is love, and all the emotions that come from love. We experience both emotions, but the one that predominates in everyday people is fear. We can say that the normal kind of relationship in this world is based 95 percent on fear and 5 percent on love. Of course, this will change depending upon the people, but even if fear is 60 percent and love is 40 percent, still it is based on fear.

In order to understand these emotions, we can describe certain characteristics about love and fear that I call the "track of love" and "the track of fear." These two tracks are merely points of reference to see how we are living our life. These divisions are for the logical mind to understand and to try to have some control of the choices we make. Let's look at some of the characteristics of love and of fear.

Love has no obligations. Fear is full of obligations. In the track of fear, whatever we do is because we *have* to do it, and we expect other people to do something because they *have* to do it. We have the obligation, and as soon we *have* to, we resist it. The more resistance we have, the more we suffer. Sooner or later, we try to escape our obligations. On the other hand, love has no resistance. Whatever we do is because we *want* to do it. It becomes a pleasure; it's like a game, and we have fun with it.

Love has no expectations. Fear is full of expectations. With fear we do things because we expect that we have to, and we expect that others are going to do the same. That is why fear hurts and love doesn't hurt. We expect something and if it doesn't happen, we feel hurt — it isn't fair. We blame others for not fulfilling our expectations. When we love, we don't have expectations; we do it because we want to, and if other people do it or not, it's because they want to or not and it's nothing personal. When we don't expect something to happen, if nothing happens, it's not important. We don't feel hurt, because whatever happens is okay. That is why hardly anything hurts us when we are in love; we aren't *expecting* that our lover will do something, and we have no obligations.

Love is based on respect. Fear doesn't respect anything, including itself. If I feel sorry for you, it means I don't respect you. You cannot make your own choices. When I have to make the choices for you, at that point I don't respect you. If I don't respect you, then I try to control you. Most of the time when we tell our children how to live their lives, it's because we don't respect them. We feel sorry for them, and we try to do for them what they should do for themselves. When I don't respect myself, I feel sorry for myself, I feel I'm not good enough to make it in this world. How do you know when you don't respect yourself? When you say, "Poor me, I'm not strong enough, I'm not intelligent enough, I'm not beautiful enough, I cannot make it." Self-pity comes from disrespect.

Love is ruthless; it doesn't feel sorry for anyone, but it does have compassion. Fear is full of pity; it feels sorry for everyone. You feel sorry for me when you don't respect me, when you don't think I am strong enough to make it. On the other hand, love respects. I love you; I know you can make it. I know you are strong enough, intelligent enough, good enough that you can make your own choices. I don't have to make your choices for you. You can make it. If you fall, I can give you my hand, I can help you to stand up. I can say, "You can do it, go ahead." That is compassion, but it is not the same as feeling sorry. Compassion comes from respect and from love; feeling sorry comes from a lack of respect and from fear.

Love is completely responsible. Fear avoids responsibility, but this doesn't mean that it's not responsible. Trying to avoid responsibility is one of the biggest mistakes we make because every action has a consequence. Everything we think, everything we do, has a consequence. If we make a choice, we have an outcome or a reaction. If we don't make a choice, we have an outcome or a reaction. We are going to experience the consequence of our actions in one way or another.

That is why every human is completely responsible for his actions, even if he doesn't want to be. Other people can try to pay for your mistakes, but you will pay for your mistakes anyway, and then you pay double. When others try to be responsible for you, it only creates a bigger drama.

Love is always kind. Fear is always unkind. With fear we are full of obligations, full of expectations, with no respect, avoiding responsibility, and feeling sorry. How can we feel good when we are suffering from so much fear? We feel victimized by everything; we feel angry or sad or jealous or betrayed.

Anger is nothing but fear with a mask. Sadness is fear with a mask. Jealousy is fear with a mask. With all those emotions that come from fear and create suffering, we can only pretend to be kind. We are not kind because we don't feel good, we are not happy. If you are in the track of love, you have no obligations, no expectations. You don't feel sorry for yourself or for your partner. Everything is going well for you, and that is why that smile is always on your face. You are feeling good about yourself, and because you are happy, you are kind. Love is always kind, and that kindness makes you generous and opens all the doors. Love is generous. Fear is selfish; it is only about me. Selfishness closes all the doors.

Love is unconditional. Fear is full of conditions. In the track of fear, I love you *if* you let me control you, *if* you are good to me, *if* you fit into the image I make for you. I create an image of the way you should be, and because you are not and never will be the image, I judge you because of that, and find you guilty. Many times I even feel ashamed of you because you are not what I want you to be. If you don't fit that image I create, you embarrass me, you annoy me, I have no patience at all with you. I am just pretending kindness. In the track of love, there is no *if*; there are no conditions. I love you for no reason, with no justi-fication. I love you the way you are, and you are free to be the way you are. If I don't like the way you are, then I'd better be with someone who is the way I like her to be. We don't have the right to change anyone else, and no one else has the right to change us. If we are going to change, it is because we want to change, because we don't want to suffer any longer.

Most people live their entire lives in the track of fear. They are in a relationship because they feel they *have* to be. They are in a relationship where they have all those expectations about their partner and about themselves. All that drama and suffering is because we are using the channels of communication that existed before we were born. People judge and are victimized, they gossip about each other, they gossip with their friends, they gossip in a bar. They make their family members hate each other. They accumulate emotional poison, and they send it to their children. "Look at your father, what he did to me. Don't be like your father. All men are like this; all women are like that." This is what we do with the people we love so much — with our own children, with our own friends, with our partners.

In the track of fear we have so many conditions, expectations, and obligations that we create a lot of rules just to protect ourselves against emotional pain, when the truth is that there shouldn't be any rules. These rules affect the quality of the channels of communication between us, because when we are afraid, we lie. If you have the expectation that I have to be a certain way, then I feel the obligation to be that way. The truth is I am not what you want me to be. When I am honest and I am what I am, you are already hurt, you are mad. Then I lie to you, because I am afraid of your judgment. I am afraid you are going to blame me, find me guilty, and punish me. And every time you remember, you punish me again and again and again for the same mistake.

In the track of love, there is justice. If you make a mistake, you pay only once for that mistake, and if you truly love yourself, you learn from that mistake. In the track of fear, there is no justice. You make yourself pay a thousand times for the same mistake. You make your partner or your friend pay a thousand times for the same mistake. This creates a sense of injustice and opens many emotional wounds. Then, of course, you set yourself up to fail. Humans have dramas for everything, even for something so simple and so little. We see these dramas in normal relationships in hell because couples are in the track of fear.

꙳

In every relationship there are two halves of that relationship. One half is you, and the other half is your son, your daughter, your father, your mother, your friends, your partner. Of those halves, you are only responsible for your half; you are not responsible for the other half. It doesn't matter how close you think you are, or how strongly you think you love, there is no way you can be responsible for what is inside another person's head. You can never know what that person feels, what that person believes, all the assumptions she makes. You don't know anything about that person. That is the truth, but what do we do? We try to be responsible for the other half, and that is why relationships in hell are based on fear, drama, and the war of control.

If we are in a war of control, it is because we have no respect. The truth is that we don't love. It is selfishness, not love; it is just to have the little doses that make us feel good. When we have no respect there is a war of control because each person feels responsible for the other. I have to control you because I don't respect you. I have to be responsible for you, because whatever happens to you is going to hurt me, and I want to avoid pain. Then, if I see that you are not being responsible, I am going to knock you all the time to try to make you be responsible, but "responsible" from my personal point of view. It doesn't mean that I am right.

This is what happens when we come from the track of fear. Because there is no respect, I act as though you are not good enough or intelligent enough to see what is good or not good for you. I make the assumption that you are not strong enough to go into certain situations and take care of yourself. I have to take control and say, "Let me do it for you," or "Don't do that." I try to suppress your half of the relationship and take control of the whole thing.

If I take control of our whole relationship, where is your part? It doesn't work.

With the other half we can share, we can enjoy, we can create the most wonderful dream together. But the other half always has its own dream, its own will, and we can never control that dream no matter how hard we try. Then we have a choice: We can create a conflict and a war of control, or we can become a playmate and a team player. Playmates and team players play together, but not against each other.

If you are playing tennis, you have a partner, you are a team, and you never go against each other — never. Even if you both play tennis differently, you have the same goal: to have fun together, to play together, to be playmates. If you have a partner who wants to control your game, and she says, "No, don't play like that; play like this. No, you are doing it wrong," you are not going to have any fun. Eventually, you won't want to play with that partner anymore. Instead of being a team, your partner wants to control how you play. And without the concept of a team, you are always going to have conflict. If you see your partnership, your romantic relationship, as a team, everything will start to improve. In a relationship, as in a game, it's not about winning or losing. You are playing because you want to have fun.

In the track of love, you are giving more than taking. And of course, you love yourself so much that you don't allow selfish people to take advantage of you. You are not going for revenge, but you are clear in your communication. You can say, "I don't like it when you try to take advantage of me, when you disrespect me, when you are unkind to me. I don't need someone to abuse me verbally, emotionally, physically. I don't need to hear you cursing all the time. It's not that I am better than you; it's because I love beauty. I love to laugh; I love to have fun; I love to love. It's not that I am selfish, I just don't need a big victim near me. It doesn't mean that I don't love you, but I cannot take responsibility for your dream. If you are in a relationship with me, it will be so hard for your Parasite, because I will not react to your garbage at all." This is not selfishness; this is self-love. Selfishness, control, and fear will break almost any relationship. Generosity, freedom, and love will create the most beautiful relationship: an ongoing romance.

✿

To master a relationship is all about you. The first step is to become aware, to know that everyone dreams his own dream. Once you know this, you can be responsible for your half of the relationship, which is you. If you know that you are only responsible for half of the relationship, you can easily control your half. It is not up to us to control the other half. If we respect, we know that our partner, or friend, or son, or mother, is completely responsible for his or her own half. If we respect the other half, there is always going to be peace in that relationship. There is no war.

Next, if you know what is love and what is fear, you become aware of the way you communicate your dream to others. The quality of your communication depends upon the choices you make in each moment, whether you tune your emotional body to love or to fear. If you catch yourself in the track of fear, just by having that awareness, you can shift your attention into the track of love. Just by seeing where you are, just by changing your attention, everything around you will change.

Finally, if you are aware that no one else can make you happy, and that happiness is the result of love coming out of you, this becomes the greatest mastery of the Toltec, the Mastery of Love.

We can talk about love and write a thousand books about it, but love will be completely different for each of us because we have to experience love. Love is not about concepts; love is about action. Love in action can only produce happiness. Fear in action can only produce suffering.

The only way to master love is to practice love. You don't need to justify your love, you don't need to explain your love; you just need to practice your love. Practice creates the master.

# 5

## The Perfect Relationship

You cannot change other people. You love them the way they are or you don't. You accept them the way they are or you don't. To try to change them to fit what you want them to be is like trying to change a dog for a cat, or a cat for a horse. That is a fact. They are what they are; you are what you are.

# 5

# The Perfect Relationship

IMAGINE A PERFECT RELATIONSHIP. YOU ARE ALWAYS intensely happy with your partner because you live with the perfect woman or man for you. How would you describe your life with this person?

Well, the way you relate with this person will be exactly the way you relate with a dog. A dog is a dog. It doesn't matter what you do, it's going to be a dog.

You are not going to change a dog for a cat or a dog for a horse; it is what it is.

Just accepting this fact in your relations with other humans is very important. You cannot change other people. You love them the way they are or you don't. You accept them the way they are or you don't. To try to change them to fit what you want them to be is like trying to change a dog for a cat, or a cat for a horse. That is a fact. They are what they are; you are what you are. You dance or you don't dance. You need to be completely honest with yourself — to say what you want, and see if you are willing to dance or not. You must understand this point, because it is very important. When you truly understand, you are likely to see what is true about others, and not just what you want to see.

If you own a dog or a cat, think about how you relate to your pet. Let's consider your relationship with a dog, for example. The animal knows how to have a perfect relationship with you. When your dog does something wrong, what do you do with your dog? A dog doesn't care what you do; it just loves you.

It doesn't have any expectations. Isn't that wonderful? But what about your girlfriend, your boyfriend, your husband, or your wife? They have so many expectations, and they are changing all the time.

The dog is responsible for its half of the relationship with you. One half of the relationship is completely normal — the dog's half. When you come home, it barks at you, it wags his tail, it pants because it is so happy to see you. It does its part very well, and you know it is the perfect dog. Your part is almost perfect also. You handle your responsibility; you feed your dog; you take care of your dog; you play with your dog. You love your dog unconditionally; you will do almost anything for your dog. You do your part perfectly, and your dog does its part perfectly.

Most people can easily imagine this kind of relationship with their dog, but why not with a woman or with a man? Do you know any woman or any man who is not perfect? The dog is a dog, and that is okay with you. You don't need to be responsible for your dog, to make it be a dog. The dog doesn't try to make you be a good human, a good master. Then why can't we allow a woman to be a woman or a man to be a man and love that human just the way he or she is without trying to change that person?

Perhaps you are thinking, "But what if I am not with the right woman or the right man?" That is a very important question. Of course, you have to choose the right woman or the right man. And what is the right woman, the right man? Someone who wants to go in the same direction as you do, someone who is compatible with your views and your values — emotionally, physically, economically, spiritually.

How do you know if your partner is right for you? Let's imagine that you are a man and a woman is going to choose you. If there are a hundred women looking for a man, and each will look at you as a possibility, for how many of these women will you be the right man? The answer is: *You don't know.* That is why you need to explore and take the risk. But I can tell you that the right woman for you is the woman you love just the way she is, the woman you don't have the need to change at all. That's the right woman for you. You are lucky if you find the right woman for you and at the same time you are the right man for her.

You are going to be the right man for her if she loves you just the way you are and she doesn't want to change you. She doesn't have to be responsible for you; she can trust that you are going to be what you claim you are, what you project you are. She can be as honest as possible and project to you what she is. She will not come to you pretending to be something that you later discover she is not. The one who loves you, *loves you just the way you are.* Because if someone wants to change you, it means you are not what that person wants. Then why is she with you?

You know, it's easy to love your dog because your dog doesn't have opinions about you. The dog loves you unconditionally. This is important. Then if your partner loves you just the way you are, it is just like the dog loves you. You can be yourself with your partner; you can be a man, or you can be a woman, just the way the dog can be a dog with you.

When you meet a person, just after the "hello," she starts sending you information right away. She can hardly wait to share her dream with you. She opens herself even if she doesn't know she is doing it. It is so easy for you to see every person just the way she is. You don't need to lie to yourself. You can see what it is you are buying, and you either want it or you don't. But you cannot blame the other person for being a dog, or a cat, or a horse. If you want a dog, then why you are getting a cat? If you want a cat, why would you get a horse or a chicken?

You know the kind of man or woman that you want? The one who makes your heart sing, the one who is aligned with the way you are, the one who loves you just as you are. Why set yourself up for something else? Why not get what you want? Why pretend to make someone fit what she is not? It doesn't mean you don't love her. It means you make a choice and say yes or no, because you love yourself also. You make a choice, and you are responsible for your choices. Then if the choices are not working well, you do not blame yourself. You simply make another choice.

But let's imagine that you get a dog and you love cats. You want your dog to behave like a cat, and you try to change the dog because it never says, "Meow." What are you doing with a dog? Get a cat! This is the only way to begin a great relationship. First you have to know what you want, how you want it, when you want it. You have to know exactly what the needs of your body are, what the needs of your mind are, and what fits well with you.

There are millions of men and women, and each one is unique. Some will make a good match for you, and some won't make a good match at all. You can love everyone; but to deal with a person on an everyday basis, you will need someone more closely aligned to you. That person doesn't need to be exactly like you; the two of you only need to be like a key in the lock — a match that works.

You need to be honest with yourself, and honest with everyone else. Project what you feel you really are, and don't pretend to be what you are not. It's as if you are in a market: You are going to sell yourself, and you are also going to buy. In order to buy, you want to see the quality of what you are going to get. But in order to sell, you need to show others what you are. It isn't about being better or worse than someone else; it's about being what you are.

If you see what you want, why not take a risk? But if you see it is not what you want, you know you are going to pay for it. Don't go around crying, "My lover abuses me," when it was so clear for you to see. Don't lie to yourself. Don't invent in people what is not there. This is the message. If you know what you want, you will find it is just like your relationship with your dog, but better.

See what is in front of you; don't be blind or pretend to see what is not there. Don't deny what you see just to get the merchandise when that merchandise will not fit your needs. When you buy something you don't need, it ends up in the garage. It's the same in a relationship. Of course, it can take years for us to learn this painful lesson, but this is a good beginning. If you make a good beginning, the rest is going to be easier because you can be yourself.

Perhaps you already have a certain amount of time invested in a relationship. If you choose to keep going, you can still have a new beginning by accepting and loving your partner just as she is. But first you will need to take a step back. You have to accept yourself and love yourself just the way you are. Only by loving and accepting yourself the way you are can you truly be and express what you are. You are what you are, and that is all you are. You don't need to pretend to be something else. When you pretend to be what you are not, you are always going to fail.

Once you accept yourself just the way you are, the next step is to accept your partner. If you decide to be with a person, don't try to change anything about her. Just like your dog or your cat, let her be who she is. She has the right to be who she is; she has a right to be free. When you inhibit your partner's freedom, you inhibit your own because you have to be there to see what your partner is doing or not doing. And if you love yourself so much, you are never going to give up your personal freedom.

Can you see the possibilities a relationship offers? Explore the possibilities. Be yourself. Find a person who matches with you. Take the risk, but be honest. If it works, keep going. If it doesn't work, then do yourself and your partner a favor: Walk away; let her go. Don't be selfish. Give your partner the opportunity to find what she really wants, and at the same time give yourself the opportunity. If it's not going to work, it is better to look in a different direction. If you cannot love your partner the way she is, someone else can love her just as she is. Don't waste your time, and don't waste your partner's time. This is respect.

If you are the provider and your partner is the addict, and this is not what you want, perhaps you would be happier with someone else. But if you decide to be in that relationship, do your best. Do your best because you are the one who is going to reap the reward. If you can love your partner the way she is, if you can open your heart completely to your partner, you can reach heaven through your love.

If you already have a cat and you want a dog, what

can you do? You can start practicing from this point forward. You have to aim for a new beginning by cutting your ties with the past and starting all over again. You don't have to have attachments to the past. All of us can change, and it can be for better. This is a new beginning for you to forgive whatever happened between you and your partner. Let it go because it was nothing but personal importance. It was nothing but misunderstanding. It was nothing but someone being hurt and trying to get even. It's not worth whatever happened in the past to spoil the possibility that you can reach heaven in a relationship. Have the courage to go for it 100 percent or let it go. Let go of the past and begin every day at a higher level of love. This will keep the fire alive and make your love grow even more.

Of course, you need to look at what it means to have the good moments and the bad moments. If being emotionally or physically abused is a bad moment, I don't know if a couple should keep going. If a bad moment is that someone loses her job, something is wrong at work, or someone has an accident, that is another kind of bad moment. If the bad moments come from fear, if they come from a lack of respect, humiliation, or hatred, I don't know how many bad moments a couple can survive.

In the relationship with your dog, you can have a bad moment. For whatever reason, it happens — an accident, a bad day at work, or whatever. You come home, and the dog is there barking at you, tail wagging, looking for your attention. You don't feel like playing with the dog, but the dog is there. The dog will not feel hurt that you don't want to play, because it doesn't take it personally. Once the dog celebrates your arrival and finds out you don't want to play, the dog goes and plays by itself. The dog doesn't stay there and insist that you be happy.

Sometimes you can feel more support from your dog than from a partner who wants to make you happy. If you don't feel like being happy, and you only want to be quiet, it's nothing personal. It has nothing to do with your partner. Perhaps you have a problem and you need to be quiet. But that silence can cause your partner to make a lot of assumptions: "What did I do now? It's because of me." It has nothing to do with your partner; it's nothing personal. Left alone, the tension will go away, and you will return to happiness.

That is why the key in the lock has to be a match, because if one of you has a bad moment or an emotional crisis, your agreement is to allow each other to be what you are. Then the relationship is another story; it's another way of being, and the whole thing can be very beautiful.

Relationship is an art. The dream that two create is more difficult to master than one. To keep the two of you happy, you have to keep your half perfect. You are responsible for your half, and your half has a certain amount of garbage. Your garbage is your garbage. The one who has to deal with that garbage is you, not your partner. If your partner tries to clean your garbage, she is going to end up with a broken nose. We have to learn not to put our nose where no one wants it.

And it's the same with your partner's half. Your partner has a certain amount of garbage. Knowing your partner has garbage, you allow her to deal with her own garbage. You are going to love her and accept her with all of her garbage. You are going to respect her garbage. You are not in the relationship to clean your partner's garbage; she is going to clean her own.

Even if your partner asks for your help, you have the choice to say no. Saying no doesn't mean you don't love or accept your partner; it means you are not able or you don't want to play that game. For example, if your partner gets angry, you can say, "You have the right to be mad, but I don't have to be mad because you are mad. I didn't do anything to cause your anger." You don't have to accept your partner's anger at all, but you can allow her to be angry. There is no need to argue; just allow her to be what she is, allow her to heal without intervening. And you can also agree not to interfere with your own healing process.

Let's say that you are a man and you are happy, and for whatever reason, your partner cannot be happy. She has personal problems; she is dealing with her garbage, and she is unhappy. Because you love her you will support her, but supporting her doesn't mean you are going to be unhappy because she's unhappy. This is not support at all. If she's unhappy and you get unhappy, both of you sink. If you are happy, your happiness can bring her happiness back.

In the same way, if you are down and she is happy, her happiness is your support. For your own sake, let her be happy; don't even try to take her happiness away. Whatever happens in your work, don't come home and throw your poison at her. Be silent and let her know it's nothing personal, you're just dealing with yourself. You can say, "Keep being happy, keep playing, and I will join you when I can enjoy your happiness. Right now, I need to be alone."

If you understand the concept of the wounded mind, you will understand the reason why romantic relationships are so difficult. The emotional body is sick. It has wounds; it has poison. If we are not aware that we are sick or that our partner is sick, we become selfish. The wounds hurt, and we have to protect our wounds, even from the one we love. But if we have the awareness, we can have different agreements. When we are aware that our partner has emotional wounds, and we love our partner, we certainly don't want to touch her wounds. We don't want to push her to heal her wounds, and we don't want her to push us to heal our wounds.

Take the risk and take the responsibility to make a new agreement with your partner — not an agreement that you read in a book, but an agreement that works for you. If it doesn't work, change that agreement and create a new one. Use your imagination to explore new possibilities, to create new agreements based on respect and love. Communication through respect and love is the whole key to keeping the love alive and never getting bored in your relationship. It's about finding your voice and stating your needs. It's about trusting yourself and trusting your partner.

What you are going to share with your partner is not the garbage, but your love, your romance, your understanding. The goal is for the two of you to be happier and happier, and that calls for more and more love. You are the perfect man or woman, and your partner is the perfect human, just as the dog is the perfect dog. If you treat your partner with love and respect, who is going to get the benefit? No one else but you.

Heal your half, and you are going to be happy. If you can heal that part of you, then you are going to be ready for a relationship without fear, without need. But remember, you can only heal your half. If you are in a relationship and you work with your half, and your partner works with the other half, you will see how quickly progress is made. Love is what makes you happy, and if you become the servant of love, and your partner becomes the servant of love, you can just imagine all the possibilities. The day will come when you can be with your partner with no guilt and no blame, no anger and no sadness. That day will be wonderful when you can be completely open, only to share, only to serve, only to give your love.

Once you decide to be a couple, you are there to serve the one you love, the one you choose. You are there to serve your love to your lover, to be each other's servant. In every kiss, in every touch, you feel you are each there to please the one you love, without expecting anything back. More than sex, it's about being together. The sex becomes wonderful also, but it's completely different. Sex becomes a communion; sex becomes a complete surrendering, a dance, an art, a supreme expression of beauty.

You can make an agreement that says, "I like you; you are wonderful and you make me feel so good. I'll bring the flowers, you bring the soft music. We'll dance, and we'll both go to the clouds." It's beautiful, it's wonderful, it's romantic. It's no longer a war of control; it's about service. But you can only do that when the love you have for yourself is very strong.

# 6

## The Magical Kitchen

Your heart is like a magical kitchen. If you open your heart, you already have all the love you need. But if you are starving for love, and you taste that love, you are going to do whatever you can for that love. You can even be so needy that you give your whole soul just for a little attention.

# 6

# The Magical Kitchen

IMAGINE THAT YOU HAVE A MAGICAL KITCHEN IN your home. In that magical kitchen, you can have any food you want from any place in the world in any quantity. You never worry about what to eat; whatever you wish for, you can have at your table. You are very generous with your food; you give your food unconditionally to others, not because you want something in return from them. Whoever comes to your home, you feed just for the pleasure of sharing your food, and your house is always full of people who come to eat the food from your magical kitchen.

Then one day someone knocks at your door, and it's a person with a pizza. You open the door, and the person looks at you and says, "Hey, do you see this pizza? I'll give you this pizza if you let me control your life, if you just do whatever I want you to do. You are never going to starve because I can bring pizza every day. You just have to be good to me."

Can you imagine your reaction? In your kitchen you can have the same pizza — even better. Yet this person comes to you and offers you food, *if* you just do whatever he wants you to do. You are going to laugh and say, "No, thank you! I don't need your food; I have plenty of food. You can come into my house and eat whatever you want, and you don't have to do anything. Don't believe I'm going to do whatever you want me to do. No one will manipulate me with food."

Now imagine exactly the opposite. Several weeks

have gone by, and you haven't eaten. You are starving, and you have no money in your pocket to buy food. The person comes with the pizza and says, "Hey, there's food here. You can have this food if you just do what I want you to do." You can smell the food, and you are starving. You decide to accept the food and do whatever that person asks of you. You eat some food, and he says, "If you want more, you can have more, but you have to keep doing what I want you to do."

You have food today, but tomorrow you may not have food, so you agree to do whatever you can for food. You can become a slave because of food, because you need food, because you don't have it. Then after a certain time you have doubts. You say, "What am I going to do without my pizza? I cannot live without my pizza. What if my partner decides to give the pizza to someone else — *my* pizza?"

Now imagine that instead of food, we are talking about love. You have an abundance of love in your heart. You have love not just for yourself, but for the whole world. You love so much that you don't need anyone's love. You share your love without condition; you don't love *if*. You are a millionaire in love, and someone knocks on your door and says, "Hey, I have love for you here. You can have my love, if you just do whatever I want you to do."

When you are full of love, what is going to be your reaction? You will laugh and say, "Thank you, but I don't need your love. I have the same love here in my heart, even bigger and better, and I share my love without condition."

But what is going to happen if you are starving for love, if you don't have that love in your heart, and someone comes and says, "You want a little love? You can have my love if you just do what I want you to do." If you are starving for love, and you taste that love, you are going to do whatever you can for that love. You can even be so needy that you give your whole soul just for a little attention.

Your heart is like that magical kitchen. If you open your heart, you already have all the love you need. There's no need to go around the world begging for love: "Please, someone love me. I'm so lonely, I'm not good enough for love; I need someone to love me, to prove that I'm worthy of love." We have love right here inside us, but we don't see this love.

Can you see the drama humans create when they believe they don't have love? They are starving for love, and when they taste a little love from someone else, that creates a big need. They become needy and obsessive about that love. Then comes the big drama: "What am I going to do if he leaves me?" "How can I live without her?" They cannot live without the provider, the one who provides them with the everyday doses. And for that little piece of love, because they are starving, they allow other people to control their lives. They let others tell them what to do, what not to do, how to dress, how not to dress, how to behave, how not to behave, what to believe, what not to believe. "I love you if you behave in this way. I love you if you let me control your life. I love you only if you are good to me. If not, then forget it."

The problem with humans is that they don't know they have a magical kitchen in their heart. All this suffering begins because long ago we closed our hearts and we no longer feel the love that is there. At some point in our life, we became afraid to love, because we believed love isn't fair. Love hurts. We tried to be good enough for someone else, we tried to be accepted by someone else, and we failed. We have already had two or three lovers and a few broken hearts. To love again is to risk too much.

Of course, we have so many self-judgments that we can't possibly have any self-love. And if there's no love for ourselves, how can we even pretend that we share love with someone else?

When we go into a relationship, we become selfish because we are needy. It's all about me. We are so self-ish that we want the person with whom we are sharing our life to be as needy as we are. We want "someone who needs me" in order to justify our existence, in order to feel that we have a reason to be alive. We think we are searching for love, but we are searching for "someone who needs me," someone we can control and manipulate.

There is a war of control in human relationships because we were domesticated to compete for the control of the attention. What we call love — someone who needs me, someone who cares about me — isn't love; it is selfishness. How can that work? Selfishness doesn't work because there is no love there. Both people are starving for love. In the sex they have, they taste a little love and it becomes addictive because they are starving for love. But then all the judgments are there. All the fear. All the blame. All the drama.

Then we search for advice on love and sex. So many books are written about it, and just about all these books could be called "How to Be Sexually Selfish." The intent is good, but where is love? They are not about learning to love; there is nothing to learn about love. Everything is already there in our genes, in our nature. We don't have to learn anything, except what we invent in this world of illusion. We search for love outside ourselves when love is all around us. Love is everywhere, but we don't have the eyes to see. Our emotional body is no longer tuned to love.

We are so afraid to love because it isn't safe to love. The fear of rejection frightens us. We have to pretend to be what we are not; we try to be accepted by our partner when we don't accept ourselves. But the problem is not that our partner rejects us. The problem is that we reject ourselves, because we are not good enough, because that is what we *believe*.

Self-rejection is the main problem. You are never going to be good enough for yourself when the idea of perfection is completely wrong. It's a false concept; it's not even real. But you believe it. Not being perfect, you reject yourself, and the level of self-rejection depends upon how strong the adults were in breaking your integrity.

After domestication, it is no longer about being good enough for anyone else. You are no longer good enough for yourself, because the big Judge is always there, reminding you that you are not perfect. As I said before, you can never forgive yourself for not being what you wish to be, and that's the real problem. If you can change that, you take care of your half of the relationship. The other half is not your problem.

If you tell someone you love him, and that person says, "Well, I don't love you," is that a reason for you to suffer? Just because someone rejects you doesn't mean you have to reject yourself. If one person doesn't love you, someone else will love you. There is always someone else. And it's better to be with someone who *wants* to be with you than to be with someone who *has* to be with you.

You have to focus on the most wonderful relationship you can have: the relationship with yourself. It is not about being selfish; it is about self-love. These are not the same. You are selfish with yourself because there is no love there. You need to love yourself, and the love will grow more and more. Then, when you enter a relationship, you don't go into it because you need to be loved. It becomes a choice. You can choose someone if you want to, and you can see who he really is. When you don't need his love, you don't have to lie to yourself.

You are complete. When love is coming out of you, you are not searching for love because you are afraid to be alone. When you have all that love for yourself, you can be alone and there's no problem. You are happy to be alone, and to share is also fun.

If I like you and we go out together, is it because we want to be jealous, because I have a need to control you, or you have a need to control me? If it's going to be that way, it isn't fun. If I'm going to be criticized or judged, if I am going to feel bad, then no thank you. If I am going to suffer, maybe it's better to be alone. Do people get together to have a drama, to possess each other, to punish each other, to be saved? Is that really why they get together? Of course, we have all those choices. But what are we really looking for?

When we are children — five, six, or seven years old — we are attracted to other children because we want to play, we want to have fun. We don't spend time with another child because we want to fight or have a big drama. That can happen, but it's going to be short-lived. We just keep playing and playing. When we get bored, we change the game, we change the rules, but we are exploring all the time.

If you go into a partnership to have drama, because you want to be jealous, because you want to be possessive, because you want to control your partner's life, you are not looking for fun, you are looking for pain, and that is what you are going to find. If you go into a relationship with selfishness, expecting that your partner is going to make you happy, it will not happen. And it's not that person's fault; it's your own.

When we go into a relationship of any kind, it is because we want to share, we want to enjoy, we want to have fun, we don't want to be bored. If we look for a partner, it is because we want to play, we want to be happy and enjoy what we are. We don't choose a partner just to give that person we claim to love all our garbage, to put all our jealousy, all our anger, all our selfishness onto that person. How can someone tell you, "I love you," and then mistreat you and abuse you, humiliate you, and disrespect you? That person may claim to love you, but is it really love? If we love, we want the best for those we love. Why put our garbage onto our own children? Why abuse them because we are full of fear and emotional poison? Why blame our parents for our own garbage?

People learn to become selfish and to close their hearts so tightly. They are starving for love, not knowing that the heart is a magical kitchen. *Your* heart is a magical kitchen. Open your heart. Open your magical kitchen, and refuse to walk around the world begging for love. In your heart is all the love you need. Your heart can create any amount of love, not just for yourself, but for the whole world. You can give your love with no conditions; you can be generous with your love because you have a magical kitchen in your heart. Then all those starving people who believe the heart is closed will always want to be near you for your love.

What makes you happy is love coming out of you. And if you are generous with your love, everyone is going to love you. You are never going to be alone if you are generous. If you are selfish, you are always going to be alone, and there is no one to blame but you. Your generosity will open all the doors, not your selfishness.

Selfishness comes from poverty in the heart, from the belief that love is not abundant. We become selfish when we believe that maybe tomorrow we won't have any pizza. But when we know that our heart is a magical kitchen, we are always generous, and our love is completely unconditional.

# 7

# The Dream Master

Your life is the manifestation of your personal dream. If you can transform the program of your personal dream, you can become a dream master. A dream master creates a masterpiece of life. But to master the dream is a big challenge because humans become slaves of their own dreams.

7

# The Dream Master

EVERY RELATIONSHIP IN YOUR LIFE CAN BE HEALED, every relationship can be wonderful, but it's always going to begin with you. You need to have the courage to use the truth, to talk to yourself with the truth, to be completely honest with yourself. Perhaps you don't have to be honest with the whole world, but you can be honest with yourself. Perhaps you cannot control what is going to happen around you, but you can control your own reactions. Those reactions are going to guide the dream of your life, your personal dream. It's your reactions that make you so unhappy or make you so happy.

Your reactions are the key to having a wonderful life. If you can learn to control your own reactions, then you can change your routines, and you can change your life.

You are responsible for the consequences of whatever you do, think, say, and feel. Perhaps it's hard for you to see what actions caused the consequence — what emotions, what thoughts — but you can see the consequence because you are suffering the consequence or enjoying the consequence. You control your personal dream by making choices. You have to see if you like the consequence of your choices or not. If it's a consequence you enjoy, then keep doing what you are doing. Perfect. But if you don't like what is happening in your life, if you aren't enjoying your dream, then try to find out what is causing the consequences you don't like. This is the way to transform your dream.

Your life is the manifestation of your personal dream. If you can transform the program of your personal dream, you can become a dream master. A dream master creates a masterpiece of life. But to master the dream is a big challenge because humans become slaves of their own dreams. The way we learn to dream is a setup. With all the beliefs we have that nothing is possible, it's hard to escape the Dream of Fear. In order to awake from the Dream, you need to master the Dream.

That is why the Toltec created the Mastery of Transformation, to break free of the old Dream and to create a new dream where everything is possible, including escaping from the Dream. In the Mastery of Transformation, the Toltec divide people into Dreamers and Stalkers. The Dreamers know that the dream is an illusion, and they play in that world of illusion, knowing it's an illusion. The Stalkers are like a tiger or a jaguar, stalking every action and reaction.

You have to stalk your own reactions; you have to work with yourself every moment. It takes a lot of time and courage, because it's easier to take things personally and react the way you always react. And that leads you to a lot of mistakes, to a lot of suffering and pain, because your reactions only generate more emotional poison and increase the drama.

If you can control your reactions, you will find that soon you are going to *see*, meaning to perceive things as they really are. The mind normally perceives things as they are, but because of all the programming, all the beliefs we have, we make interpretations of what we perceive, of what we hear, and mainly of what we see.

There's a big difference between seeing the way people see in the Dream, and seeing without judgment, as it is. The difference is in the way your emotional body reacts to what you perceive. For example, if you are walking on the street and someone who doesn't know you says, "You are so stupid" and walks away, you can perceive and react to that in many ways. You can accept what that person said and think, "Yes, I must be stupid." You can get mad, or feel humiliated, or simply ignore it.

The truth is that this person is dealing with his own emotional poison, and he said that to you because you were the first person to cross his path. It has nothing to do with you. There is nothing personal there. If you can see that truth, the way it is, you don't react.

You can say, "Look at that person who is suffering so much," but you don't take it personally. This is just one example, but it applies to almost everything that happens in every moment. We have a little ego that takes everything personally, that makes us over-react. We don't see what is really happening because we react right away and make it part of our dream.

Your reaction comes from a belief that is deep inside you. The way you react has been repeated thousands of times, and it becomes a routine for you. You are conditioned to be a certain way. And that is the challenge: to change your normal reactions, to change your routine, to take a risk and make different choices. If the consequence is not what you want, change it again and again until you finally get the result you want.

I have said that we never chose to have the Parasite, which is the Judge, the Victim, and the Belief System. If we know we didn't have a choice, and we have the awareness that it's nothing but a dream, we recover something very important that we lost — something that religions call "free will." Religions say that when humans were created, God gave us free will. This is true, but the Dream took it away from us and kept it, because the Dream controls the will of most humans.

There are people who say, "I want to change, I *really* want to change. There is no reason for me to be so poor. I am intelligent. I deserve to live a good life, to earn much more money than I earn." They know this, but that is what their mind is telling them. What do these people do? They go and turn the television on and spend hours and hours watching it. Then how strong is their will?

Once we have awareness, we have a choice. If we could have that awareness all the time, we could change our routines, change our reactions, and change our entire life. Once we have the awareness, we recover free will. When we recover free will, in any moment we can choose to remember who we are. Then, if we forget, we can choose again, *if* we have the awareness. But if we don't have the awareness, we have no choice.

Becoming aware is about being responsible for your own life. You are not responsible for what is happening in the world. You are responsible for yourself. You didn't make the world the way it is; the world was already the way it is before you were born. You didn't come here with a great mission to save the world, to change society, but surely you come with a big mission, an important mission. The real mission you have in life is to make yourself happy, and in order to be happy, you have to look at what you believe, the way you judge yourself, the way you victimize yourself.

Be completely honest about your happiness. Don't project a false sense of happiness by telling everyone, "Look at me. I'm a success in life, I have everything I want, I am so happy," when you don't like yourself.

Everything is there for us, but first we need to have the courage to open our eyes, to use the truth, and to see what really is. Humans are so blind, and they are blind because they don't want to see. Let's look at an example.

A young woman meets a man and she feels a strong attraction for him right away. Her hormones go all the way up, and she just wants the man. All her girlfriends can see what this man is. He's on drugs, he's not working, he's got all those traits that make a woman suffer so much. But she sees him, and what does she see? She only sees what she wants to see. She sees that he's tall, he's handsome, he's strong, he's charming. She creates an image of the man and tries to deny what she doesn't want to see. She lies to herself. She really wants to believe the relationship will work. The girlfriends say, "But he's on drugs, he's an alcoholic, he's not working." She says, "Yes, but my love is going to change him."

Of course, her mother hates the man, and the father does, too. Her parents are worried about her because they can see where she is going. They say, "This is not a good man for you." The young woman says, "You are telling me what to do." She goes against Mom and against Dad to follow her hormones, and she lies to herself trying to justify her choices. "It's my life, and I'm going to do whatever I want to do."

Months later, the relationship brings her back to reality. The truth starts coming out, and she blames the man for what she didn't want to see before. There's no respect, there's a lot of abuse, but now her pride is more important. How can she go back home when Mom and Dad were right? That will only give them satisfaction. How long will it take for this woman to learn the lesson? How much does she love herself? What is the limit of her self-abuse?

All that suffering occurs because we don't want to see, when it is so clear before our eyes. Even when we meet someone and he tries to pretend to be the best he can, even with that false mask, he cannot avoid presenting the lack of love, the lack of respect he has. But we don't want to see it and we don't want to hear.

That is why an ancient prophet once said, "There is no worse blind man than the one who doesn't want to see. There is no worse deaf man than the one who doesn't want to hear. And there is no worse madman than the one who doesn't want to understand."

We are so blind, we really are, and we pay for that. But if we open our eyes and see life as it is, we can avoid a lot of emotional pain. It doesn't mean we don't take a risk. We are alive and we need to take risks, and if we fail, so what? Who cares? It doesn't matter. We learn and we move on without judgment.

We don't need to judge; we don't need to blame or feel guilt. We just need to accept our truth and intend a new beginning. If we can see ourselves the way we are, that is the first step toward self-acceptance — toward stopping the self-rejection. Once we are able to accept ourselves just the way we are, everything can start changing from that point forward.

Everyone has a price, and Life respects that price. But that price is not measured in dollars or in gold; it is measured in love. More than that, it is measured in self-love. How much you love yourself — that is your price — and Life respects the price. When you love yourself, your price is very high, which means your tolerance for self-abuse is very low. It's very low because you respect yourself. You like yourself the way you are, and this makes your price higher. If you don't like things about yourself, the price is a little lower.

Sometimes the self-judgment is so strong that people need to be numb just to be with themselves. If you don't like a person, you can walk away from that person. If you don't like a group of people, you can walk away from those people. But if you don't like yourself, it doesn't matter where you go, you are right there. To avoid being with yourself, you need to take something to numb you, to take your mind away from yourself. Perhaps some alcohol is going to help. Perhaps some drugs will help. Perhaps eating — just eat, eat, eat. The self-abuse can get much worse. There are people who really feel self-hatred. They are self-destructive, killing themselves little by little, because they don't have the courage to kill themselves fast.

If you observe self-destructive people, you will see they attract people just like them. What do we do if we don't like ourselves? We try to get numb with alcohol to forget our suffering. That's the excuse we use. Where are we going to get alcohol? We go to a bar to drink, and guess who's going to be there? People just like us, who try to avoid themselves also, who also try to get numb. We get numb together, we start talking about our suffering, and we understand each other very well. We even start to enjoy it. We understand each other perfectly because we vibrate in the same frequency. We are both being self-destructive. Then I hurt you, you hurt me — a perfect relationship in hell.

What happens when you change? For whatever reason, you no longer need the alcohol. It's okay now to be with yourself, and you really enjoy it. You no longer drink, but you have the same friends, and everyone's drinking. They get numb, they start getting happier, but you can clearly see that their happiness is not real. What they call happiness is a rebellion against their own emotional pain. In that "happiness" they are so hurt that they have fun hurting other people and hurting themselves.

You no longer fit in, and of course they resent you because you are no longer like them. "Hey, you are rejecting me because you no longer drink with me, because you don't get high with me." Now you have to make a choice: You can step back, or you can go to another level of frequency and meet people who finally accept themselves like you do. You find there is another realm of reality, a new way of relationship, and you no longer accept certain kinds of abuse.

# 8

## Sex: The Biggest Demon in Hell

Humans accumulate a lot of knowledge; we learn all those beliefs, morals, and rules from our family, society, religion. And we base most of our behavior, most of our feelings, on that knowledge. We create angels and demons, and of course, sex becomes the biggest demon in hell.

# 8

# Sex: The Biggest Demon in Hell

IF WE COULD TAKE HUMANS OUT OF THE CREATION of the universe, we would see that the whole creation — the stars, the moon, the plants, the animals, everything — is perfect just the way it is. Life doesn't need to be justified or judged; without us, it keeps going the way it is. If you put humans in that creation, but take away the ability to judge, you will find we are exactly like the rest of nature. We are not good or bad or right or wrong; we are just the way we are.

In the Dream of the Planet, we have the need to justify everything — to make everything good or bad or right or wrong, when it is just the way it is, period. Humans accumulate a lot of knowledge; we learn all those beliefs, morals, and rules from our family, society, religion. And we base most of our behavior, most of our feelings, on that knowledge. We create angels and demons, and of course, sex becomes the biggest demon in hell. Sex is the biggest sin of the humans, when the human body is made for sex.

You are a biological, sexual being, and that is just the way it is. Your body is so wise. All that intelligence is in the genes, in the DNA. The DNA doesn't need to understand or justify everything; it just knows. The problem is not with sex. The problem is the way we manipulate the knowledge and our judgments, when there is really nothing to justify. It's so hard for the mind to surrender, to accept that it's just the way it is. We have a whole set of beliefs about what sex should be, about how relationships should be, and these beliefs are completely distorted.

In hell, we pay a high price for a sexual encounter, but the instinct is so strong that we do it anyway. Then we have all that guilt, all that shame; we hear all that gossip about sex. "Look at what this woman is doing, ooh! Look at that man." We have a whole definition of what a woman is, what a man is, how a woman should behave sexually, how a man should behave sexually. Men are always too macho or too wimpy depending on who is judging. Women are always too thin or too fat. We have all these beliefs about how a woman should be in order to be beautiful. You have to buy the right clothes, create the right image, so you can be seductive and fit that image. If you don't fit that image of beauty, you grow up believing that you're not worthy, that no one will like you.

We believe so many lies about sex that we don't enjoy sex. Sex is for animals. Sex is evil. We should be ashamed to have sexual feelings. These rules about sex go completely against nature, and it's just a dream, but we believe it. Your true nature comes out and it doesn't fit with all those rules. You are guilty. You are not what you should be. You are judged; you are victimized. You punish yourself, and it's not fair. This creates wounds that become infected with emotional poison.

The mind plays this game, but the body doesn't care what the mind believes; the body just feels the sexual need. At a certain time in our lives, we cannot avoid feeling sexual attraction. This is completely normal; it is not a problem at all. The body is going to feel sexual when it's excited, when it's touched, when it's visually stimulated, when it sees the possibility of sex. The body can feel sexual, and a few minutes later, stop feeling sexual. If the stimulation ends, the body stops feeling the need for sex, but the mind is another story.

Let's say that you are married and were raised as a Catholic. You have all those ideas about how sex should be — about what is good or bad or right or wrong, about what is a sin and what is acceptable. You need to sign a contract to make sex okay; if you don't sign the contract, sex is a sin. You have given your word to be loyal, but one day you are walking on the street and a man crosses in front of you. You feel a strong attraction; the *body* feels the attraction. There is no problem, it doesn't mean you will take any action, but you cannot avoid the feeling because it's completely normal. When the stimulation is gone, the body lets go, but the mind needs to justify what the body feels.

The mind *knows,* and that's the problem. Your mind knows, *you* know, but what is it that you know? You know what you believe. It doesn't matter if it's good or bad, right or wrong, correct or incorrect. You are raised to believe this is bad, and right away you make that judgment. Now the drama and conflict begin.

Later you think of that man, and just thinking of him makes your hormones go up again. Because of the powerful memory that's in the mind, it's as if your body is seeing him again. The body reacts because the mind thinks about it. If the mind would leave the body alone, that reaction would go away as if it never happened. But the mind remembers it, and because you know it's not okay, you start to judge yourself. The mind says it's not okay and tries to repress what it feels. When you try to repress your mind, guess what? You think about it more. Then you see that man, and even if it's in a different situation, your body reacts more strongly.

If the first time you had just let go of the judgment, perhaps you would see him the second time and you would have no reaction at all. Now you see the man, you have sexual feelings, and you judge these feelings and think, "Oh my God, it's not okay. I'm a terrible woman." You need to be punished; you are guilty; you are going in a downward spiral, and for nothing, because it's all in the mind. Perhaps that man doesn't even notice that you exist. You start imagining the whole thing, you make assumptions, and you start to want him more. For whatever reason you meet the man, you talk to him, and it's beautiful for you. It becomes an obsession, it's very attractive, but you are afraid.

Then you make love to him, and it's the greatest thing and the worst thing at the same time. Now you really need to be punished. "What kind of woman would allow her sexual desire to be greater than her morals?" Who knows what games the mind is going to play. You hurt, but you try to deny your feelings; you try to justify your actions to avoid the emotional pain. "Well, my husband is probably the same way."

The attraction becomes stronger, but it's not because of your body; it's because the mind is playing a game. The fear becomes an obsession, and all that fear you have about your sexual attraction is building up. When you make love with this man, you have a great experience, but not because he is great, and not because the sex was great, but because all the tension, all the fear, is released. To build it up again, the mind plays the game that it's because of that man, but it isn't true.

The drama keeps growing, and it's nothing but a simple mental game. It's not even real. It's not love either, because this kind of relationship becomes very destructive. It is self-destructive, because you are hurting yourself, and the place that hurts most is what you believe. It doesn't matter if your belief is right or wrong or good or bad, you are breaking your beliefs, which is something that we wish to do, but in the way of the spiritual warrior, not the way of the victim. Now you are going to use that experience to go deeper into hell, not to get out of hell.

❧

Your mind and your body have completely different needs, but your mind has control of your body. Your body has needs that you cannot avoid; you have to fulfill the need for food, the need for water, shelter, sleep, sex. All those needs of your body are completely normal, and it's so easy to satisfy the needs of the body. The problem is that the mind says these are *my* needs.

In the mind we create a whole picture in this bubble of illusion, and the mind takes responsibility for everything. The mind thinks it has the need for food, for water, for shelter, for clothing, for sex. But the mind has no needs at all, no physical needs. The mind doesn't need food, doesn't need oxygen, doesn't need water, doesn't need sex at all. How do we know this is true? When your mind says, "I need food," you eat, and the body is completely satisfied, but your mind still thinks it needs food. You keep eating and eating and eating, and you cannot satisfy your mind with food, because that need is not real.

The need to cover your body is another example. Yes, your body needs to be covered because the wind is too cold or because the sun is too hot, but it's your body that has the need and it's so easy to satisfy the need. When the need is in the mind, you can have tons of clothes and the mind still needs clothes. You open the closet and it's full of clothes, but your mind isn't satisfied. What does it say? "I have nothing to wear."

The mind needs another car, another vacation, a guest house for your friends — all those needs that you never can fully satisfy are in the mind. Well, it's the same with sex. When the need is in the mind, you cannot satisfy the need. When the need is in the mind, the whole judgment, the whole knowledge, is also there. This makes sex so difficult to deal with. The mind doesn't need sex. What the mind really needs is love, not sex. More than the mind, it's your soul that needs love, because your mind can survive with fear. Fear is energy also, and it's food for the mind — not exactly the food you want, but it works.

We need to give the body the freedom from the tyrant that is the mind. If we no longer have the need for food in our mind, the need for sex in our mind, everything becomes so easy. The first step is to split the needs into two categories: These are the needs of the body; these are the needs of the mind.

The mind confuses the needs of the body with its own needs because the mind needs to know: *What am I?* We live in this world of illusion, and we have no idea what we are. The mind creates all these questions. *What am I?* becomes the biggest mystery, and any answer satisfies the need to feel safe. The mind says, "I am the body. I am what I see; I am what I think; I am what I feel. I am hurting; I am bleeding."

The affinity between the mind and the body is so close that the mind believes, "I am the body." The body has a need, and the mind says, "I need." The mind takes everything about the body personally because it tries to understand *What am I?* So it is completely normal that the mind starts to gain control of the body at a certain point. And you live your life until something happens that shakes you and allows you to see what you are not.

You start to become aware when you see what you are not, when your mind starts to realize that it is not the body. Your mind says, "Then what am I? Am I the hand? If I cut off my hand, I am still me. Then I am not the hand." You take away what is not you, until in the end the only thing that remains is what you really are. It's a long process of the mind finding its own identity. In the process, you let go of the personal story, what makes you feel safe, until finally you understand what you really are.

You find out that you are not what you believe you are, because you never chose your beliefs. These beliefs were there when you were born. You find out that you are also not the body, because you start to function without your body. You start to notice that you are not the dream, that you are not the mind. If you go deeper, you start noticing that you are not the soul either. Then what you find out is so incredible. You find out that what you are is a *force* — a force that makes it possible for your body to live, a force that makes it possible for your whole mind to dream.

Without you, without this force, your body would collapse on the floor. Without you, your whole dream just dissolves into nothing. What you really are is that force that is *Life*. If you look into the eyes of someone near you, you will see the self-awareness, the manifestation of Life, shining in his eyes. Life is not the body; it is not the mind; it is not the soul. It is a force. Through this force, a newborn baby becomes a child, a teenager, an adult; it reproduces and grows old. When Life leaves the body, the body decomposes and turns to dust.

You are Life passing through your body, passing through your mind, passing through your soul. Once you find that out, not with the logic, not with the intellect, but because you can *feel* that Life — you find out that you are the force that makes the flowers open and close, that makes the hummingbird fly from flower to flower. You find out that you are in every tree, you are in every animal, vegetable, and rock. You are that force that moves the wind and breathes through your body. The whole universe is a living being that is moved by that force, and that is what you are. *You are Life.*

# 9

## The Divine Huntress

Humans hunt for love. ... We hunt for love in other humans just like us, expecting to get love from them when these humans are in the same condition as we are. They don't love themselves either, so how much love can we get from them?

9

# The Divine Huntress

IN GREEK MYTHOLOGY THERE IS A STORY ABOUT
Artemis, the divine huntress. Artemis was the supreme
huntress because the way she hunted was effortless.
She fulfilled her needs so easily and lived in perfect
harmony with the forest. Everything in the forest
loved Artemis, and to be hunted by her was an honor.
It never seemed like Artemis was hunting; whatever

she needed came to her. That is why she was the best hunter, but this also made her the most difficult prey. Her animal form was a magical deer that was almost impossible to hunt.

Artemis lived in perfect harmony in the forest, until one day a king gave an order to Hercules, the son of Zeus, who was searching for his own transcendence. The order was that Hercules had to hunt the magical deer of Artemis. Hercules, being the undefeated son of Zeus, did not refuse; he went to the forest to hunt the deer. The deer saw Hercules, and she wasn't afraid of him. She let Hercules come close, but when Hercules tried to capture her, she ran. There was no way Hercules could get this deer unless he became a better hunter than Artemis.

Hercules called upon Hermes, the messenger of the Gods, the fastest one, to lend him his wings. Now Hercules was as fast as Hermes, and soon the most valuable prey was in the hands of Hercules. You can imagine the reaction of Artemis. She was hunted by Hercules, and of course she wanted to get even. She wanted to hunt Hercules, and she did her best to capture him, but Hercules was now the most difficult prey. Hercules was so free and although she tried and tried, Artemis could not capture him.

Artemis didn't need Hercules at all. She felt a strong need to have him, but of course it was only an illusion. She believed she was in love with Hercules, and she wanted him for herself. The one thing on her mind was to get Hercules, and it became an obsession until she was no longer happy. Artemis started to change. She was no longer in harmony with the forest because now she hunted just for the pleasure of getting the prey. Artemis broke her own rules and became a predator. The animals were afraid, and the forest started to reject her, but Artemis didn't care. She didn't see the truth; she only had Hercules on her mind.

Hercules had many works to do, but sometimes he would go to the forest to visit Artemis. Every time he did, Artemis did her best to hunt him. When she was with Hercules, she felt so happy to be with him, but she knew he would leave, and she became jealous and possessive. Every time Hercules left, she suffered and she cried. She hated Hercules, but she loved him also.

Hercules had no idea what was going on in the mind of Artemis; he didn't notice she was hunting him. In his mind, he was never the prey. Hercules loved and respected Artemis, but this is not what she wanted. Artemis wanted to own him; she wanted to hunt him and be the predator with him. Of course everyone in the forest noticed the difference in Artemis except her. In her mind she was still the divine huntress. She didn't have the awareness that she had fallen. She wasn't aware that the heaven that was the forest had become hell, because after her fall, the rest of the hunters fell with her; they all became predators.

One day Hermes took an animal form, and just as Artemis was ready to destroy Hermes, he became a God and she rediscovered the wisdom she had lost. He let her know she had fallen, and with this awareness Artemis went to Hercules to ask for his forgiveness. It was nothing but her personal importance that brought her to that fall. In talking to Hercules she realized she had never offended him because he didn't know what was going on in her mind. Then she looked around the forest and she saw what she had done to the forest. She apologized to every flower and to every animal until she recovered love. Once again, Artemis became the divine huntress.

I tell this story to let you know that all of us are hunters, and all of us are prey. Everything that exists is both hunter and prey. What is it that we hunt? We hunt to fulfill our needs. I have talked about the needs of the body versus the needs of the mind. When the mind believes it is the body, the needs are only illusions, and they cannot be fulfilled. When we hunt those needs that are unreal in the mind, we become the predators — we are hunting for what we don't need.

Humans hunt for love. We feel that we need that love because we believe we don't have love, because we don't love ourselves. We hunt for love in other humans just like us, expecting to get love from them when these humans are in the same condition as we are. They don't love themselves either, so how much love can we get from them? We merely create a bigger need that isn't real; we keep hunting and hunting, but in the wrong place, because other humans don't have the love we need.

When Artemis became aware of her fall, she went back to herself, because everything she needed was inside herself. It is the same for all of us, because all of us are like Artemis after she fell and before her redemption. We are hunting for love. We are hunting for justice and happiness. We are hunting for God, but God is inside us.

❧

The hunting of the magical deer teaches you that you have to hunt inside yourself. This is a great story to keep in mind. If you remember the story of Artemis, you will always find the love inside you. Humans who hunt each other for love will never be satisfied; they will never find the love they need in other humans. The mind feels the need, but we cannot fulfill it, because it isn't there. *It's never there.*

The love we need to hunt is inside ourselves, but that love is difficult prey. It is so difficult to hunt inside yourself, to get that love from inside you. You have to be very fast, as fast as Hermes, because anything can distract you from your goal. Whatever traps your attention distracts you from reaching your goal, from getting the prey that is the love inside. If you can capture the prey, you will see that your love can grow strong inside you, and it can fulfill all your needs. This is so important for your happiness.

Usually humans go into relationships as the hunter. They look for what they feel they need, hoping to find what they need in the other person, only to find that it's not there. When you enter a relationship without this need, it's a different story.

How do you hunt inside yourself? To capture the love inside yourself, you have to surrender to yourself as the hunter and the prey. Inside your own mind, there is the hunter and there is also the prey. Who is the hunter, who is the prey? In ordinary people the hunter is the Parasite. The Parasite knows everything about you, and what the Parasite wants are the emotions that come from fear. The Parasite is a garbage eater. It loves fear and drama; it loves anger, jealousy, and envy; it loves any emotion that makes you suffer. The Parasite wants to get even, and it wants to be in control.

Your self-abuse, as the Parasite, is hunting you twenty-four hours a day; it is always after you. So we become the prey of the Parasite, a very easy prey. The Parasite is the one who abuses you. It is more than a hunter; it is a predator, and it is eating you alive. The prey, the emotional body, is that part of us that suffers and suffers; it's that part of us that wants to be redeemed.

In Greek mythology, there is also the story of Prometheus, who is chained to a rock. During the day an eagle comes and eats his innards; during the night he recovers. Every day the eagle comes and eats his insides again. What does this mean? When Prometheus is awake, he has a physical and emotional body. The eagle is the Parasite that is eating his insides. During the night, he doesn't have the emotional body, and he recovers. He is born again to be the food for that eagle, until Hercules comes to release him. Hercules is like the Christ, Buddha, or Moses who breaks the chain of suffering and gives you your freedom.

To hunt inside yourself, you start by hunting every reaction you have. You are going to change one routine at a time. It is a war for freedom from the Dream that controls your life. It is a war between you and the predator with the Truth in the middle. In all the Western traditions from Canada to Argentina, we call ourselves warriors because a warrior is the hunter who hunts herself. It is a big war, because it's a war against the Parasite. To be a warrior doesn't mean you will win the war, but at least you rebel, and you no longer accept that the Parasite is eating you alive.

Becoming the hunter is the first step. When Hercules went into the forest in search of Artemis, there was no way he could capture the deer. Then he went to Hermes, the supreme teacher, and he learned to become a better hunter. He needed to be better than Artemis in order to hunt her. To hunt yourself, you also need to be a better hunter than the Parasite.

If the Parasite is working twenty-four hours a day, you also have to work twenty-four hours a day. The Parasite has an advantage: It knows you very well. There is no way you can hide. The Parasite is the most difficult prey. It's that part of you that tries to justify your behavior in front of other people, but when you are alone, it is the worst judge. It is always judging, blaming, and making you feel guilty.

In a normal relationship in hell, the Parasite of your partner allies with your Parasite against the real you. You have against yourself not just your own Parasite, but the Parasite of your partner, who aligns with your Parasite to make the suffering eternal. If you know that, you can make a difference. You can have more compassion for your partner and allow her to deal with her own Parasite. You can be happy every time your partner takes another step toward freedom. You can be aware that when your partner gets upset, gets sad or jealous, it's not the one you love that you are dealing with at that moment. It's a Parasite that is possessing your partner.

Knowing the Parasite is there, and knowing what is going on in your partner, you can give your partner the space to deal with it. Since you are only responsible for your half of the relationship, you can allow her to deal with her own personal dream. In that way, it will be easy not to take personally what your partner is doing. This will help your relationship a lot, because nothing that your partner does is personal. Your partner is dealing with her own garbage. If you don't take it personally, it will be so easy for you to have a wonderful relationship with your partner.

# 10

## Seeing With Eyes of Love

You could say that the eyes are an expression of what you feel. . . . When you are angry, you see the world with eyes of anger. . . . If you are sad, you see with the eyes of sadness, and everything you perceive will be sad. But if you have the eyes of love, you just see love wherever you go.

# 10

## Seeing With Eyes of Love

IF YOU LOOK AT YOUR BODY, YOU WILL FIND billions of living beings who depend on you. Every cell in your body is a living being that depends on you. You are responsible for all of those beings. For all those living beings that are your cells, you are God. You can provide what they need; you can love all those living beings, or you can be so mean to them.

The cells in your body are completely loyal to you; they work for you in harmony. We can even say they pray to you. You are their God. That is absolutely the truth. Now what are you going to do with this knowledge?

Remember, the whole forest was in complete harmony with Artemis. When Artemis fell, she lost respect for the whole forest. When she recovered her awareness, Artemis went from flower to flower to say, "I am sorry; now I will take care of you again." And the relationship between Artemis and the forest became a love relationship again.

The whole forest is your body, and if you just acknowledge this truth, you will say to your body, "I am sorry; now I will take care of you again." The relationship between you and your body, between you and all those living cells that depend on you, can become the most beautiful relationship. Your body and all those living cells are perfect in their half of the relationship, just like the dog is perfect in its half. The other half is your mind. Your body takes care of its half of the relationship, but the mind is the one that abuses the body, that mistreats the body, that gets so mean with the body.

Just look at the way you treat your cat or your dog. If you can treat your body the same way you treat your pet, you will you see that it's about love. Your body is willing to receive all the love from the mind, but the mind says, "No, I don't like this part of my body. Look at my nose; I don't like my nose. My ears — they are too large. My body is too fat. My legs are too short." The mind can imagine all kinds of things about the body.

Your body is perfect the way it is, but we have all those concepts about right and wrong, good and bad, beautiful and ugly. These are just concepts, but we believe them, and that's the problem. With the image of perfection we have in our mind, we expect our body to look a certain way, to act a certain way. We reject our own body when the body is completely loyal to us. Even when our body can't do something because of its limitations, we push our body and our body at least tries.

Look at what you do with your own body. If you reject your own body, what can other people expect from you? If you accept your own body, you can accept almost everyone, almost everything. This is a very important point when it comes to the art of relationship. The relationship you have with yourself is reflected in your relationships with others. If you reject your own body, when you are sharing your love with your partner, you become shy. You think, "Look at my body. How can he love me when I have a body like this?" Then you reject yourself and make the assumption that the other person will reject you for the same thing you reject in yourself. And when you reject someone else, you reject him for the same things you reject in yourself.

To create a relationship that takes you all the way to heaven, you have to accept your body completely. You have to love your body and allow your body to be free to just be, to be free to give, free to receive, without being shy, because "shy" is nothing but fear.

Imagine how you see your pet dog. You see the dog with eyes of love and you enjoy the beauty of that dog. It doesn't make any difference whether that dog is beautiful or ugly. You can go into ecstasy just seeing the beauty of that dog, because it's not about possessing beauty. Beauty is just a concept we learned.

Do you think a turtle or a frog is ugly? You can see a frog, and the frog is beautiful; it's gorgeous. You can see a turtle, and it's beautiful. Everything that exists is beautiful — everything. But you think, "Oh, that is ugly," because someone made you believe what is ugly and what is beautiful, just as someone made you believe what is good and what is bad.

There's no problem at all with being beautiful or ugly, short or tall, thin or heavy. There's no problem with being gorgeous. If you walk through a crowd of people, and they tell you, "Oh, you are beautiful," you can say, "Thank you, I know," and keep going. It doesn't make any difference to you. But it will make a difference to you if you don't believe you are beautiful and someone tells you that. Then you are going to say, "Am I really?" This opinion can impress you, and, of course, that makes you easy prey.

This opinion is what you think you need, because you believe you are not beautiful. Remember the story of the Magical Kitchen? If you have all the food you need, and someone asks you to let him control you for food, you say, "No, thank you." If you wish to be beautiful, but you don't believe you are, and someone says, "I will always tell you how beautiful you are if you just let me control you," you will say, "Oh yes, please tell me I'm beautiful." You are going to allow that to happen because you think you need that opinion.

What is important are not all those opinions from others, but your own opinions. You are beautiful no matter what your mind tells you. That is a fact. You don't have to do anything because you already have all the beauty you need. To be beautiful you don't have any obligation to anyone. Others are free to see whatever they want to see. If others see you and judge you beautiful or not, if you are aware of your own beauty and accept your own beauty, their opinion doesn't affect you at all.

Perhaps you grew up believing that you are unattractive and you envy beauty in others. Then to justify the envy, you tell yourself, "I don't want to be beautiful." You may even have a fear of being beautiful. This fear can come from many directions, and it's not the same for everyone, but often it is the fear of your own power. Women who are beautiful have power over men, and not just over men, but over women. Other women who are not as beautiful as you are, may envy you because you attract the attention of men. If you dress a certain way and all the men are crazy about you, what are the women going to say about you? "Oh, she's a loose woman." You become afraid of all those judgments people have about you. This is nothing but concepts again, nothing but false beliefs that open wounds in the emotional body. Then, of course we have to cover these wounds with lies and denial systems.

Envy is also a belief that can easily be broken with awareness. You can learn to deal with the envy of other women or other men because the truth is that each of you is beautiful. The only difference between the beauty of one person and the beauty of another is the concept of beauty that people have.

Beauty is nothing but a concept, nothing but a belief, but you can believe in that concept of beauty, and base all your power on that beauty. Time passes, and you see you are getting old. Perhaps you are not as beautiful as you were from your point of view, and a younger woman comes along who is now the one who is beautiful. Time for plastic surgery, to try to keep the power because we believe that our beauty is our power. Our own aging starts to hurt us. "Oh my god, my beauty is going away. Will my man still love me if I am not as attractive? Now he can see other women who are more attractive than me."

We resist aging; we believe that because someone is old, it means she is not beautiful. This belief is completely wrong. If you see a newborn baby, it is beautiful. Well, an old person is also beautiful. The problem is the emotion we have in our eyes to perceive what is and what is not beautiful. We have all these judgments, all these programs that put limits on our own happiness, that push us to self-rejection and to reject other people also. Can you see how we play the drama, how we set ourselves up to fail with all these beliefs?

Aging is something beautiful, just as growing up is beautiful. We grow from a child, to a teenager, to a young woman or a young man. It is beautiful. To become an old woman or an old man is also beautiful. In the life of humans, there are certain years when we actively reproduce. During those years, we may want to be sexually attractive, because nature makes us that way. After that, we don't have to be sexually attractive from that point of view, but it does not mean we are not beautiful.

You are what you believe you are. There is nothing to do except to be just what you are. You have the right to feel beautiful and enjoy it. You can honor your body and accept it as it is. You don't need anyone to love you. Love comes from the inside. It lives inside us and is always there, but with that wall of fog, we don't feel it. You can only perceive the beauty that lives outside you when you *feel* the beauty that lives inside you.

You have a belief about what is beautiful and what is ugly, and if you don't like yourself, you can change your belief and your life will change. It sounds simple, but it isn't easy. Whoever controls the belief, controls the dream. When the dreamer finally controls the dream, the dream can become a masterpiece of art.

୧ଡ଼

You can begin by doing a *puja* for your body every day. In India, people perform pujas, or rituals, for the different Gods and Goddesses. In the puja, they bow to the idol, they put flowers near the idol, and they feed the idol with all their love, because these statues represent God. Every day, you can offer a devotional love to your own body. When you take a shower, when you take a bath, treat your body with all your love, treat your body with honor, with gratitude, with respect. When you eat, take a bite, close your eyes, and enjoy the food. That food is an offering to your own body, to the temple where God lives. Do this every day, and you will feel your love for your body growing stronger each day, and you will never again reject yourself.

Just imagine how you will feel the day you adore your own body. When you accept yourself completely, you will feel so good about your own body, and you are going to be so happy. Then when you relate with someone else, your limit of self-abuse is almost zero. This is self-love. This is not personal importance because you treat others with the same love, the same honor, the same respect, and the same gratitude you use with yourself. Can you see the perfection in a relationship like that? It's about honoring the God inside each other.

When you make it your goal to create the perfect relationship between you and your body, you are learning to have a perfect relationship with anyone you are with, including your mother, your friends, your lover, your children, your dog. When you have the perfect relationship between you and your body, in that moment your half of any relationship outside you is completely fulfilled. You no longer depend upon the success of a relationship from the outside.

When you do a puja with your own body, when you know how to have that devotion for your own body, and you touch your lover's body, you touch it with the same devotion, the same love, the same honor, the same gratitude. And when your lover touches your body, it's completely open; there is no fear, there is no need — it is full of love.

Imagine all the possibilities in sharing your love this way. You don't even need to touch. Just looking into each other's eyes is enough to fulfill the needs of the mind and the needs of the soul. The body is already satisfied because it has all your love. You are never lonely anymore, because you are fulfilled with your own love.

Wherever you turn your face, you will be fulfilled by love, but not from other humans. You can see a tree and feel all the love coming from the tree to you. You can see the sky, and it's going to fulfill the needs of your mind for love. You will see God everywhere, and it will no longer be just a theory. *God is everywhere. Life is everywhere.*

Everything is made by *Love*, by *Life*. Even fear is a reflection of love, but fear exists in the mind, and in humans, that fear controls the mind. Then we interpret everything according to what we have in our mind. If we have fear, what we perceive will be analyzed with fear. If we are mad, what we perceive will be perceived according to anger. Our emotions act like a filter through which we see the rest of the world.

You could say that the eyes are an expression of what you feel. You perceive the outside Dream according to your eyes. When you are angry, you see the world with eyes of anger. If you have eyes of jealousy, your reactions will be different, because the way you see the world is through jealousy. When you have the eyes of madness, everything will bother you. If you have the eyes of sadness, you are going to cry because it's raining, because there is noise, because of everything. Rain is rain. There is nothing to judge or interpret, but you are going to see the rain according to your emotional body. If you are sad, you see with the eyes of sadness, and everything you perceive will be sad.

But if you have the eyes of love, you just see love wherever you go. The trees are made with love. The animals are made with love. The water is made with love. When you perceive with the eyes of love, you can connect your will with the will of another dreamer, and the dream becomes one. When you perceive with love, you become one with the birds, with nature, with a person, with everything. Then you can see with the eyes of an eagle or transform into any kind of life. With your love you connect with the eagle and you become the wings, or you become the rain, or the clouds. But to do this, you need to clean the mind of fear and perceive with eyes of love. You have to develop your will until it is so strong that it can hook the other will and become one will. Then you have wings to fly. Or being the wind, you can come here, you can go there, you can push away the clouds and the sun is shining. This is the power of love.

When we fulfill the needs of our mind and our body, our eyes see with love. We see God everywhere. We even see God behind the Parasite of other people.

Inside every human is the Promised Land that Moses promised his people. That Promised Land is in the realm of the human mind, but only the mind that is fertile for Love, because that is where God lives. If you see the ordinary human mind, it is also a fertile land, but for the Parasite that grows the seeds of envy, anger, jealousy, and fear.

In the Christian tradition, you hear of Gabriel coming with the trumpet for the Resurrection, and everyone comes out of his grave to live the Eternal Life. That grave is the Parasite and the Resurrection is the return to *Life*, because you are alive only when your eyes can see *Life*, which is *Love*.

You can have a relationship that fulfills your dream of Heaven; you can create a Paradise, but you have to begin with you. Begin with complete acceptance of your body. Hunt the Parasite, and make it surrender. Then the mind will love your body and will no longer sabotage your love. It's up to you; it's not up to anyone else. But first, you are going to learn how to heal your emotional body.

# 11

# Healing the Emotional Body

The truth is like a scalpel because it is painful to open our wounds and uncover all of the lies. The wounds in our emotional body are covered by the denial system, the system of lies we have created to protect those wounds. When we look at our wounds with eyes of truth, we can finally heal them.

# 11

## Healing the Emotional Body

LET'S IMAGINE AGAIN THAT WE HAVE A SKIN disease with wounds that are infected. When we want to heal the skin, and we go to a doctor, the doctor is going to use a scalpel to open the wounds. Then the doctor is going to clean the wounds, apply medicine, and keep the wounds clean until they heal and no longer hurt us.

To heal the emotional body, we are going to do the same thing. We need to open the wounds and clean the wounds, use some medicine, and keep the wounds clean until they heal. How are we going to open the wounds? We are going to use the truth as a scalpel to open the wounds. Two thousand years ago, one of the greatest Masters told us, "And you will know the truth, and the truth will set you free."

The truth is like a scalpel because it is painful to open our wounds and uncover all of the lies. The wounds in our emotional body are covered by the denial system, the system of lies we have created to protect those wounds. When we look at our wounds with eyes of truth, we can finally heal them.

You begin by practicing the truth with yourself. When you are truthful with yourself, you start to see everything as it is, not the way you want to see it. Let's use an example that is emotionally charged: rape.

Let's say that someone raped you ten years ago, and it is true that you were raped. Right now, it is no longer true. It was a dream, and in that dream someone abused you with violence. You didn't look for that. It was nothing personal. For whatever reason, it happened to you and can happen to anyone. But by being raped, will you condemn yourself to suffer in your sexuality for the rest of your life? The rapist is not condemning you to do that. You are the victim, and if you judge yourself and find yourself guilty, for how many years will you punish yourself by not enjoying something that is one of the most beautiful things in the world? Sometimes being raped can destroy your sexuality for the rest of your life. Where is the justice? You are not the rapist, so why should you suffer the rest of your life for something you didn't do? You are not guilty for being raped, but the Judge in your mind can make you suffer and live in shame for many years.

Of course, this injustice will create a strong emotional wound and a lot of emotional poison that could take years of therapy to be released. The truth is that, yes, you were raped, but it's no longer true that you must suffer this experience. That is a choice.

This is the first step in using the truth as a scalpel: You find that the injustice that created a wound is no longer true, right now, in this moment. You discover that perhaps what you *believe* hurt you so badly was never true. Even if it was true, it doesn't mean that *now* it is true. By using the truth, you open the wound and see the injustice from a new perspective.

The truth is relative in this world; it's changing all the time because we live in a world of illusions. What is true right now is not true later. Then it could be true again. The truth in hell could also be just another concept, another lie that can be used against you. Our own denial system is so powerful and strong that it becomes very complicated. There are truths covering lies, and lies covering truth. Like peeling an onion, you uncover the truth little by little until in the end, you open your eyes to find out that everyone around you, including yourself, is lying all the time.

Almost everything in this world of illusion is a lie. That is why I ask my apprentices to follow three rules for seeing what is true. The first rule is: *Don't believe me.*

You don't have to believe me, but think, and make choices. Believe what you want to believe according to what I say, but only if it makes sense for you, if it makes you happy. If it guides you into your awakening, then make the choice to believe it. I am responsible for what I say, but I am not responsible for what you understand. We live in a completely different dream. What I say, even if it is absolutely true for me, is not necessarily true for you. The first rule is very easy: *Don't believe me.*

Rule number two is more difficult: *Don't believe yourself.* Don't believe all the lies you tell yourself — all those lies that you never chose to believe, but were programmed to believe. Don't believe yourself when you say you are not good enough, you are not strong enough, you are not intelligent enough. Don't believe your own boundaries and limitations. Don't believe you are unworthy of happiness or love. Don't believe you are not beautiful. Don't believe whatever makes you suffer. Don't believe in your own drama. Don't believe in your own Judge or your own Victim. Don't believe the inner voice that tells you how stupid you are, that tells you to kill yourself. Don't believe it, because it isn't true. Open your ears, open your heart, and listen. When you hear your heart guiding you to your happiness, then make a choice and stick to it. But don't believe yourself just because you say so, because more than 80 percent of what you believe is a lie — it isn't *true*. The second rule is a difficult one: *Don't believe yourself.*

Rule number three is: *Don't believe anyone else.* Don't believe other people because they are lying all the time anyway. When you no longer have emotional wounds, when you don't have the need to believe other people just to be accepted, you see everything more clearly. You see if it is black or white, if it is or is not. What is right now, maybe in a few moments is not. What is not right now, maybe in a few moments will be. Everything is changing so fast, but if you are aware, you can see the change. Don't believe others because they will use your own stupidity to manipulate your mind. Don't believe anyone who says she comes from Pleiades and she wants to save the world. Bad news!

We don't need anyone to come and save the world. The world doesn't need the aliens to come from the outside to save us. The world is alive; it's a living being, and it's more intelligent than all of us together. If we believe the world needs to be saved, soon someone will come and say, "Okay, a comet is coming, we need to escape from the planet. Kill yourself and boom! You will reach the comet and go to heaven." Don't believe these mythologies. You create your own dream of heaven; no one can create it for you. Nothing but common sense will guide you to your own happiness, your own creation. Rule number three is difficult because we have the need to believe other people. *Don't believe them.*

Don't believe me, don't believe yourself, and don't believe anyone else. By not believing, whatever is untrue will disappear like smoke in this world of illusion. Everything is what it is. You don't need to justify what is true; you don't need to explain it. What is true doesn't need anyone's support. Your lies need your support. You need to create a lie to support the first lie, another lie to support that lie, and more lies to support all of those lies. You create a big structure of lies, and when the truth comes out, everything falls apart. But that's just the way it is. You don't need to feel guilty because you are lying.

Most of the lies we believe simply dissipate if we don't believe them. Whatever is not true will not survive skepticism, but the truth will always survive skepticism. What is truth is true, believe it or not. Your body is made of atoms. You don't have to believe it. Believe it or not, it is true. The universe is made of stars; this is true, believe it or not. Only what is true will survive, and that includes the concepts you have about yourself.

We have said that when we were children, we didn't have the opportunity to choose what to believe and what not to believe. Well, now it is different. Now that we are grown, we have the power to make a choice. We can believe or not believe. Even if something is not the truth, if we choose to believe it, we can believe it just because we *want* to believe it. You can choose how you want to live your life. And if you are honest with yourself, you will know you are always free to make new choices.

When we are willing to see with eyes of truth, we uncover some of the lies and open the wounds. Still, there is the poison inside the wounds.

Once we open the wounds, we are going to clean the wounds of all the poison. How are we going to do this? The same Master gave us the solution two thousand years ago: Forgiveness. There is no other way but forgiveness to clean the wounds of all the poison.

You must forgive those who hurt you, even if whatever they did to you is unforgivable in your mind. You will forgive them not because they deserve to be forgiven, but because you don't want to suffer and hurt yourself every time you remember what they did to you. It doesn't matter what others did to you, you are going to forgive them because you don't want to feel sick all the time. Forgiveness is for your own mental healing. You will forgive because you feel compassion for yourself. Forgiveness is an act of self-love.

Let's take an example of a divorced woman. Imagine you have been married for ten years, and for whatever reason you have a big fight with your husband over a big injustice. You get divorced, and you really hate your ex-husband. Just hearing his name, you feel a strong pain in your stomach and you want to throw up. The emotional poison is so strong that you can't stand it any longer. You need help, so you go to a therapist and say, "I am suffering so much. I am full of anger, jealousy, envy. What he did is unforgivable. I hate that man."

The therapist looks at you and says, "You need to release your emotions; you need to express your anger. What you should do is have a big tantrum. Get a pillow, bite the pillow, hit the pillow, and release your anger." You go and have the biggest tantrum, and you release all these emotions. It really seems to work. You pay your therapist $100 and say, "Thank you very much. I feel much better." Finally, you have a big smile on your face.

You walk out of the therapist's office, and guess who is driving through town? As soon as you see your ex-husband, the same anger comes up, but even worse. You have to run to the therapist again and pay another $100 for another tantrum. Releasing your emotions in this way is only a temporary solution. It may release some poison and make you feel better for a while, but it does not heal the wound.

The only way to heal your wounds is through forgiveness. You have to forgive your ex-husband for the injustice. You will know you have forgiven someone when you see him and you don't feel anything anymore. You will hear the name of the person and have no emotional reaction. When you can touch a wound and it doesn't hurt, then you know you have truly forgiven. Of course, a scar is going to be there, just as it is on your skin. You will have a memory of what happened, of how you used to be, but once the wound has healed, it won't hurt you any longer.

Perhaps you are thinking, "Well, it's easy to say we should forgive. I have tried, but I cannot do it."

You have all these reasons, all these justifications why you cannot forgive. But this is not the truth. The truth is that you cannot forgive because you learned not to forgive, because you practiced not to forgive, because you mastered not to forgive.

There was a time when we were children when forgiveness was our instinct. Before we caught the mental disease, it was effortless and natural to forgive. We used to forgive others almost right away. If you see two children playing together, and they start to fight and hit each other, the children cry and run to their mothers. "Hey, she hit me!" One mother goes to talk with the other mother. The two mothers have a big fight, and five minutes later the two children are playing together again as if nothing happened. Now the mothers hate each other for the rest of their lives.

It is not that we need to learn forgiveness, because we are born with the capacity for forgiveness. But guess what happened? We learned the opposite behavior, and we practiced the opposite behavior, and now forgiveness is very difficult. Whoever does something to us, forget it, that's it, she is out of our life. It becomes a war of pride. Why? Because our personal importance grows when we don't forgive. It makes our opinion more important when we can say, "Whatever she does, I will not forgive her. What she did is unforgivable."

The real problem is pride. Because of pride, because of honor, we add more fire to the injustice to remind ourselves that we cannot forgive. Guess who is going to suffer and accumulate more and more emotional poison? We are going to suffer for all kinds of things people do around us, even though they have nothing to do with us.

We also learn to suffer just to punish whoever abused us. We behave like a little child having a tantrum, just asking for attention. I'm hurting myself just to say, "Look at what I am doing because of you." It's a big joke, but that's exactly what we do. What we really want to say is, "God, forgive me," but we will not say a word until God comes and asks us for forgiveness first. Many times we don't even know why we are so upset with our parents, our friends, our mate.

We are upset, and if for some reason the other person asks us for forgiveness, right away we start to cry and say, "Oh no, you forgive me."

Go and find the little child in the corner having a tantrum. Take your pride and put it in the trash. You don't need it. Just let go of the personal importance and ask for forgiveness. Forgive others, and you will see miracles start to happen in your life.

First, make a list of everyone you believe you need to ask for forgiveness. Then ask them for forgiveness. Even if there is not enough time to call everyone, ask for their forgiveness in your prayers and through your dreams. Second, make a list of all the people who hurt you, all the people you need to forgive. Start with your parents, your brothers and sisters, your children, your spouse, your friends, your lover, your cat, your dog, your government, and God.

Now, you are going to forgive others by knowing that whatever anyone did to you had nothing to do with you. Everyone dreams her own dream, remember? The words and actions that hurt you are merely a reaction to the demons in that person's own mind. She is dreaming in hell, and you are a secondary character in her dream. Nothing anyone does is because of you. Once you have this awareness, and you do not take it personally, compassion and understanding will lead you to forgiveness.

Start working on forgiveness; start practicing forgiveness. It will be difficult at first, but then it just becomes a habit. The only way to recover forgiveness is to practice again. You practice and practice, until in the end you see if you can forgive yourself. At a certain point, you find that you must forgive yourself for all those wounds and all that poison you created for yourself in your own dream. When you forgive yourself, self-acceptance begins and self-love grows. That is the supreme forgiveness — when you finally forgive yourself.

Create an act of power and forgive yourself for everything you have done in your whole life. And if you believe in past lives, forgive everything you believe you did in all of your past lives. The concept of karma is true only because we believe it is true. Because of our beliefs about being good and bad, we feel ashamed about what we believe is bad. We find ourselves guilty, we believe we deserve to be punished, and we punish ourselves. We have the belief that what we create is so dirty that it needs to be cleaned. And just because you believe it, then, *"Thy will be done."* It is real for you. You create your karma, and you have to pay for it. That is how powerful you are. To break old karma is simple. You just stop that belief by refusing to believe it, and the karma is gone. You don't need to suffer, you don't need to pay anything; it is over. If you can forgive yourself, the karma is gone just like that. From this point on, you can start all over again. Then life becomes easy, because forgiveness is the only way to clean the emotional wounds. Forgiveness is the only way to heal them.

Once we have cleaned the wounds, we are going to use a powerful medicine to accelerate the process of healing. Of course, the medicine also comes from the same great Master: It is Love. Love is the medicine that accelerates the process of healing. There is no other medicine but unconditional love. Not: I love you *if*, or I love myself *if*. There is no *if*. There is no justification. There is no explanation. It is just to love. Love yourself, love your neighbor, and love your enemies. This is simple, common sense, but we cannot love others until we love ourselves. That is why we must begin with self-love.

There are millions of ways to express your happiness, but there is only one way to really be happy, and that is to love. There is no other way. You cannot be happy if you don't love yourself. That is a fact. If you don't love yourself, you don't have any opportunity to be happy. You cannot share what you do not have. If you do not love yourself, you cannot love anyone else either. But you can have a need for love, and if there's someone who needs you, that's what humans call love. That is not love. That is possessiveness, that is selfishness, that is control with no respect. Don't lie to yourself; that is not love.

Love coming out of you is the only way to be happy. Unconditional love for yourself. Complete surrender to that love for yourself. You no longer resist life. You no longer reject yourself. You no longer carry all that blame and guilt. You just accept who you are, and accept everyone else the way he or she is. You have the right to love, to smile, to be happy, to share your love, and to not be afraid to receive it also.

That is the healing. Three simple points: the truth, forgiveness, and self-love. With these three points, the whole world will heal and will no longer be a mental hospital.

These three keys to heal the mind were given to us by Jesus, but he is not the only one who taught us how to heal. Buddha did the same; Krishna did the same. Many other Masters came to the same conclusions and gave us these same lessons. All around the world, from Japan to Mexico to Peru to Egypt to Greece, there were humans who were healed. They saw that the disease is in the human mind, and they used these three methods: the truth, forgiveness, and self-love. If we can see our state of mind as a disease, we find there is a cure. We don't have to suffer any longer; if we are aware that our mind is sick, that our emotional body is wounded, we can also heal.

Just imagine if all humans could start being truthful with themselves, start forgiving everyone, and start loving everyone. If all humans loved in this way, they would no longer be selfish; they would be open to give and receive, and they would no longer judge each other. Gossiping would be over, and the emotional poison would simply dissolve.

Now we are talking about a completely different Dream of the Planet. It doesn't look like the planet Earth. This is what Jesus called "Heaven on Earth," Buddha called "Nirvana," and Moses called "The Promised Land." It is a place where all of us can live in love because we put our attention on love. We choose to love.

Whatever you call the new Dream, it is still a dream as real or as false as the dream of hell. But now you can choose which dream you want to live in. Now you have the tools in your hands to heal yourself. The question is: What are you going to do with them?

# 12

## God Within You

When you know that the power that is Life is inside you, you accept your own Divinity, and yet you are humble, because you see the same Divinity in everyone else. You see how easy it is to understand God, because everything is a manifestation of God.

# 12

## God Within You

YOU ARE THE FORCE THAT PLAYS WITH YOUR mind and uses your body as its favorite toy to play and have fun with. That is the reason you are here: to play and have fun. We are born with the right to be happy, with the right to enjoy life. We are not here to suffer. Whoever wants to suffer is welcome to suffer, but we don't have to suffer.

Then why do we suffer? Because the whole world suffers, and we make the assumption that suffering is normal. Then we create a belief system to support that "truth." Our religions tell us that we came here to suffer, that life is a valley of tears. Suffer today, have patience, and when you die you will have your reward. Sounds beautiful, but it isn't true.

We choose to suffer because we learned to suffer. If we continue to make the same choices, we will continue to suffer. The Dream of the Planet carries the story of humanity, the evolution of humans, and suffering is the result of human evolution. Humans suffer because we *know*: We know what we believe, we know all those lies, and because we can't fulfill all those lies, we suffer.

It's not true that you go to hell or to heaven after you die. You live in hell or you live in heaven, but now. Heaven and hell only exist in the level of the mind. If we suffer now, when we die we still suffer, because the mind doesn't die with the brain. The dream continues and when our dream is hell, our brain dies and we are still dreaming in the same hell. The only difference between being dead and being asleep is that when we are sleeping we can awake because we have a brain. When we are dead, we cannot awake because we don't have a brain, but the dream is there.

Heaven or hell is here and now. You don't need to wait to die. If you take responsibility for your own life, for your own actions, then your future is in your hands, and you can live in heaven while the body is alive.

The dream most humans create on this planet is obviously hell. This isn't right or wrong or good or bad, and there is no one to blame. Can we blame our parents? No. They did the best they could when they programmed you as a little child. Their own parents did the same with them: the best they could. If you have children, you couldn't know what else to do either. How can you blame yourself? To become aware doesn't mean you need to blame anyone, or carry guilt for what you have done. How can we carry guilt or blame for a mental disease that is seriously contagious?

You know, everything that exists is perfect. You are perfect just the way you are. That is the truth. You are a master. Even if you master anger and jealousy, your anger and jealousy are perfect. Even if you have a big drama going on in your life, it's perfect, it's beautiful. You can go to a movie like *Gone with the Wind* and cry for all that drama. Who says that hell is not beautiful? Hell can inspire you. Even hell is perfect, because only perfection exists. Even if you dream hell in your life, you are perfect just the way you are.

It is only knowledge that makes us believe we are not perfect. Knowledge is nothing more than a description of the Dream. The Dream is not real, so knowledge isn't real either. Wherever knowledge comes from, it is only real from one point of perception. Once you shift the perception, it is no longer real. We are never going to find ourselves with our knowledge. In the end that is what we are looking for: to find ourselves, to be ourselves, to live our own life, instead of the life of the Parasite — the life we were programmed to live.

It isn't knowledge that will lead us to ourselves; it is wisdom. We have to make a distinction between knowledge and wisdom, because they are not the same.

The main way to use knowledge is to communicate with each other, to agree on what we perceive. Knowledge is the only tool we have to communicate, because humans hardly communicate heart to heart. What is important is how we use our knowledge, because we become the slaves of knowledge and we are no longer free.

Wisdom has nothing to do with knowledge; it has to do with freedom. When you are wise, you are free to use your own mind and run your own life. A healthy mind is free of the Parasite; it is free again the way it was before domestication. When you heal your mind, when you break free of the Dream, you are no longer innocent, but wise. You become just like a child again in many ways, except for one big difference: A child is innocent, and that's why he can fall into suffering and unhappiness. The one who transcends the Dream is wise; that is why she doesn't fall anymore, because now she *knows* — she also has knowledge of the Dream.

You don't need to accumulate knowledge to become wise; anyone can become wise. Anyone. When you become wise, life becomes easy, because you become who you really are. It's difficult to try to be what you are not, to try to convince yourself and everyone else that you are what you are not. Trying to be what you are not expends all your energy. Being what you are doesn't require any effort.

When you become wise, you don't have to use all those images you created; you don't have to pretend to be something else. You accept yourself the way you are, and the complete acceptance of yourself becomes the complete acceptance of everyone else. You no longer try to change other people or impose your point of view. You respect other people's beliefs. You accept your body and your own humanity with all the instincts of your body. There is nothing wrong with being an animal. We are animals, and animals always follow their instinct. We are humans, and because we are so intelligent, we learn to repress our instincts; we don't listen to what comes from the heart. That's why we go against our own body and try to repress the needs of the body or deny they exist. This is not wise.

When you become wise, you respect your body, you respect your mind, you respect your soul. When you become wise, your life is controlled by your heart, not your head. You no longer sabotage yourself, your own happiness, or your own love. You no longer carry all that guilt and blame; you no longer have all those judgments against yourself, and you no longer judge anyone else. From that moment on, all the beliefs that make you unhappy, that push you to struggle in life, that make your life difficult, just vanish.

Surrender all those ideas about being what you are not, and become what you really are. When you surrender to your nature, to what you really are, you no longer suffer. When you surrender to the real you, you surrender to Life, you surrender to God. Once you surrender, there is no longer a struggle, there is no resistance, there is no suffering.

Being wise, you always go for the easy way, which is to be yourself, whatever you are. Suffering is nothing but resistance to God. The more you resist, the more you suffer. It is simple.

Imagine that from one day to another, you awake from the Dream and you are completely healthy. You no longer have wounds, you no longer have emotional poison. Imagine the freedom you are going to experience. Everything is going to make you happy just to be alive, wherever you go. Why? Because the healthy human being is not afraid to express love. You are not afraid to be alive, and you are not afraid to love. Imagine how you would live your life, how you would treat the people you are close to, if you no longer had those wounds and that poison in your emotional body.

In the mystery schools around the world, this is called the awakening. It is as if you awake one day, and you no longer have emotional wounds. When you no longer have those wounds in the emotional body, the boundaries disappear, and you start to see everything as it is, not according to your belief system.

When you open your eyes and you don't have those wounds, you become a skeptic — not to increase your personal importance by telling everyone how intelligent you are, or to make fun of other people who believe in all those lies. No, when you awake, you become a skeptic because it's clear in your eyes that the Dream is not true. You open your eyes, you are awake, and everything becomes obvious.

When you awake, you cross a line of no return, and you never see the world in the same way. You are still dreaming — because you cannot avoid dreaming, because dreaming is the function of the mind — but the difference is that you know it's a dream. Knowing that, you can enjoy the dream or suffer the dream. That depends on you.

The awakening is like being at a party where there are thousands of people and everyone is drunk except you. You are the only sober person in the party. That is the awakening, because the truth is that most humans see the world through their emotional wounds, through their emotional poison. They don't have the awareness that they are living in a dream of hell. They aren't aware that they are living in a dream just as fish swimming in water are not aware that they are living in water.

When we awake and we are the only sober person in the party where everyone is drunk, we can have compassion because we were drunk too. We don't need to judge, not even people in hell, because we, too, were in hell.

When you awake, your heart is an expression of the Spirit, an expression of Love, an expression of Life. The awakening is when you have the awareness that *you are Life.* When you are aware that you are the force that is Life, anything is possible. Miracles happen all the time, because those miracles are performed by the heart. The heart is in direct communion with the human soul, and when the heart speaks, even with the resistance of the head, something inside you changes; your heart opens another heart, and true love is possible.

❧

There is a an old story from India about the God, Brahma, who was all alone. Nothing existed but Brahma, and he was completely bored. Brahma decided to play a game, but there was no one to play the game with.

So he created a beautiful goddess, Maya, just for the purpose of having fun. Once Maya existed and Brahma told her the purpose of her existence, she said, "Okay, let's play the most wonderful game, but you have to do what I tell you to do." Brahma agreed, and following Maya's instructions, he created the whole universe. Brahma created the sun and the stars, the moon and the planets. Then he created life on earth: the animals, the oceans, the atmosphere, everything.

Maya said, "How beautiful is this world of illusion you created. Now I want you to create a kind of animal that is so intelligent and aware that it can appreciate your creation." Finally Brahma created humans, and after he finished the creation, he asked Maya when the game was going to start.

"We will start right now," she said. She took Brahma and cut him into thousands of teeny, tiny pieces. She put a piece inside every human and said, "Now the game begins! I am going to make you forget what you are, and you are going to try to find yourself!" Maya created the Dream, and still, even today,

Brahma is trying to remember who he is. Brahma is there inside you, and Maya is stopping you from remembering what you are.

When you awake from the Dream, you become Brahma again, and reclaim your divinity. Then if Brahma inside you says, "Okay, I am awake; what about the rest of me?" you know the trick of Maya, and you can share the truth with others who are going to wake up too. Two people who are sober in the party can have more fun. Three people who are sober is even better. Begin with you. Then others will start to change, until the whole dream, the whole party, is sober.

❧

The teachings that come from India, from the Toltec, the Christians, the Greeks — from societies all over the world — come from the same truth. They talk about reclaiming your Divinity and finding God within you. They talk about having your heart completely open and becoming wise. Can you imagine what kind of world this would be if all humans opened their hearts and found the love inside? Of course we can do it. Everyone can do it in his own way. It's not about following any imposed idea; it's about finding yourself, and expressing yourself in your own particular way. That is why your life is an art. Toltec means "artist of the spirit." The Toltec are the ones who can express with the heart, the ones who have unconditional love.

You are alive because of the power of God, which is the power of Life. You are the force that is Life, but because you are able to think at the level of the mind, you forget what you really are. Then it's easy to see someone else and say, "Oh, there is God. God will be responsible for everything. God will save me." No. God has just come to tell you — to tell the God in you — to be aware, to make a choice, to have the courage to work through all your fears and change them, so you are no longer afraid of love. The fear of love is one of the biggest fears that humans have. Why? Because in the Dream of the Planet, a broken heart means "Poor me."

Perhaps you wonder, "If we are truly Life or God, why don't we know it?" Because we are programmed not to know. We are taught: "You are a human; these are your limitations." Then we limit our possibilities by our own fears. You are what you believe you are. Humans are powerful magicians. When you believe you are what you are, then that is what you are. And you can do that because you are Life, God, Intent. You have the power to make yourself what you are right now. But it's not your reasoning mind that controls your power; it's what you believe.

You see, everything is about belief. Whatever we believe rules our existence, rules our life. The belief system we create is like a little box we put ourselves inside of; we cannot escape because we believe we cannot escape. That is our situation. Humans create their own boundaries, their own limitations. We say what is humanly possible, and what is not possible. Then just because we believe it, it becomes truth for us.

The prophecies of the Toltec have foreseen the beginning of a new world, a new humanity where humans take responsibility for their own beliefs, for their own lives. The time is coming when you will become your own guru. You don't need other humans to tell you what the Will of God is. Now it's you and God face-to-face, without any intermediary. You were searching for God, and you found God within you. God is no longer there, outside you.

When you know that the power that is Life is inside you, you accept your own Divinity, and yet you are humble, because you see the same Divinity in everyone else. You see how easy it is to understand God, because everything is a manifestation of God. The body is going to die, the mind is going to dissolve also, but not you. You are immortal; you exist for billions of years in different manifestations, because you are Life, and Life cannot die. You are in the trees, the butterflies, the fish, the air, the moon, the sun. Wherever you go, you are there, waiting for yourself.

Your body is a temple, a living temple where God lives. Your mind is a living temple where God lives. God is living within you as Life. The proof that God lives within you is that you are alive. Your Life *is* the proof. Of course, in your mind there is garbage and emotional poison, but God is also there.

You don't have to do anything to reach God, to reach enlightenment, to awaken. There is no one who can take you to God. Whoever says they will take you to God is a liar, because you are already there. There's only one living being, and want it or not, resist it or not, effortlessly you are with God already.

The only thing left is to enjoy your life, to be alive, to heal your emotional body so you can create your life in such a way that you openly share all the love inside you.

The whole world can love you, but that love will not make you happy. What will make you happy is the love coming out of you. That is the love that will make a difference, not the love everyone has for you. Your love for everyone is your half; the other half can be a tree, it can be a dog, it can be a cloud. You are one half; the other half is what you perceive. You are the half as a dreamer, and the dream is the other half.

You are always free to love. If your choice is to be in a relationship, and your partner is playing the same game, what a gift! When your relationship is completely out of hell, you will love yourselves so much that you don't need each other at all. By your own will, you get together and create beauty. And what the two of you are going to create is a dream of heaven.

You have already mastered fear and self-rejection; now you are returning to self-love. You can be so strong and so powerful that with your self-love you transform your personal dream from fear to love, from suffering to happiness. Then just like the sun, you are giving light and giving love all the time, with no conditions. When you love with no conditions, you the human, and you the God, align with the Spirit of Life moving through you. Your life becomes the expression of the beauty of the Spirit. Life is nothing but a dream, and if you create your life with Love, your dream becomes a masterpiece of art.

## Prayers

Beginning today and gradually over time, help us to increase the power of our love so that we may create a masterpiece of art — our own life. Today, Creator, we give you all of our gratitude and love because you have given us Life.

Amen.

# Prayers

PLEASE TAKE A MOMENT TO CLOSE YOUR EYES, OPEN your heart, and feel all the love that is coming from your heart.

I want you to join me in a special prayer to experience a communion with our Creator.

Focus your attention on your lungs, as if only your lungs existed. Feel the pleasure when your lungs expand to fulfill the biggest need of the human body: to breathe.

Take a deep breath and feel the air as it fills your lungs. Feel how the air is made of love. Notice the connection between the air and the lungs, a connection of love. Expand your lungs with air until your body has the need to expel that air. Then exhale, and feel the pleasure again. When we fulfill any need of the human body, it gives us pleasure. To breathe gives us pleasure. Just to breathe is enough for us to always be happy, to enjoy life. Just to be alive is enough. Feel the pleasure of being alive, the pleasure of the feeling of love. . . .

## PRAYER FOR AWARENESS

Today, Creator of the Universe, we ask that you open our heart and open our eyes so we can enjoy all of your creations and live in eternal love with you. Help us to see you in everything we perceive with our eyes, with our ears, with our heart, with all our senses. Let us perceive with eyes of love so that we find you wherever we go and see you in everything you create. Let us see you in every cell of our body, in every emotion of our mind, in every dream, in every flower, in every person we meet. You cannot hide from us because you are everywhere, and we are one with you. Let us be aware of this truth.

Let us be aware of our power to create a dream of heaven where everything is possible. Help us to use our imagination to guide the dream of our life, the magic of our creation, so we can live without fear, without anger, without jealousy, without envy. Give us a light to follow, and let today be the day that our search for love and happiness is over. Today let something extraordinary happen that will change our life forever: Let everything we do and say be an expression of the beauty in our heart, always based on love.

Help us to be the way you are, to love the way you love, to share the way you share, to create a masterpiece of beauty and love, the same way that all of your creations are masterpieces of beauty and love. Beginning today and gradually over time, help us to increase the power of our love so that we may create a master-piece of art — our own life. Today, Creator, we give you all of our gratitude and love because you have given us Life. Amen.

## PRAYER FOR SELF-LOVE

Today, Creator of the Universe, we ask that you help us to accept ourselves just the way we are, without judgment. Help us to accept our mind the way it is, with all our emotions, our hopes and dreams, our personality, our unique way of being. Help us to accept our body just the way it is, with all its beauty and perfection. Let the love we have for ourselves be so strong that we never again reject ourselves or sabotage our happiness, freedom, and love.

From now on, let every action, every reaction, every thought, every emotion, be based on love. Help us, Creator, to increase our self-love until the entire dream of our life is transformed, from fear and drama to love and joy. Let the power of our self-love be strong enough to break all the lies we were pro-grammed to believe — all the lies that tell us we are not good enough, or strong enough, or intelligent enough, that we cannot make it. Let the power of our self-love be so strong that we no longer need to live our life according to other people's opinions. Let us trust ourselves completely to make the choices we must make. With our self-love, we are no longer afraid to face any responsibility in our life or face any problems and resolve them as they arise. Whatever we want to accomplish, let it be done with the power of our self-love.

Starting today, help us to love ourselves so much that we never set up any circumstances that go against us. We can live our life being ourselves and not pretending to be someone else just to be accepted by other people. We no longer need other people to accept us or tell us how good we are because we know what we are. With the power of our self-love, let us enjoy what we see every time we look in the mirror. Let there be a big smile on our face that enhances our inner and outer beauty. Help us to feel such intense self-love that we always enjoy our own presence.

Let us love ourselves without judgment, because when we judge, we carry blame and guilt, we have the need for punishment, and we lose the perspective of your love. Strengthen our will to forgive ourselves in this moment. Clean our minds of emotional poison and self-judgments so we can live in complete peace and love.

Let our self-love be the power that changes the dream of our life. With this new power in our hearts, the power of self-love, let us transform every relationship we have, beginning with the relationship we have with ourselves. Help us to be free of any conflict with others. Let us be happy to share our time with our loved ones and to forgive them for any injustice we feel in our mind. Help us to love ourselves so much that we forgive anyone who has ever hurt us in our life.

Give us the courage to love our family and friends unconditionally, and to change our relationships in the most positive and loving way. Help us to create new channels of communication in our relationships so there is no war of control, there is no winner or loser. Together let us work as a team for love, for joy, for harmony.

Let our relationships with our family and friends be based on respect and joy so we no longer have the need to tell them how to think or how to be. Let our romantic relationship be the most wonderful relationship; let us feel joy every time we share ourselves with our partner. Help us to accept others just the way they are, without judgment, because when we reject them, we reject ourselves. When we reject ourselves, we reject you.

Today is a new beginning. Help us to start our life over beginning today with the power of self-love. Help us to enjoy our life, to enjoy our relationships, to explore life, to take risks, to be alive, and to no longer live in fear of love. Let us open our heart to the love that is our birthright. Help us to become Masters of Gratitude, Generosity, and Love so that we can enjoy all of your creations forever and ever. Amen.

## About the Author

MIGUEL RUIZ IS A MASTER OF THE TOLTEC MYSTERY school tradition. For more than a decade, he has worked with a small group of students and apprentices, guiding them toward their personal freedom. For information about current programs offered by don Miguel or his apprentices, please visit us online at www.miguelruiz.com.

~

## The Sixth Sun Foundation

The Sixth Sun Foundation is a non-profit organization dedicated to empowering people to find personal freedom and happiness through the teachings brought forth by don Miguel. If you are interested in joining a Four Agreements Group to further integrate The Four Agreements into your daily life, or are interested in receiving information about our many programs, please visit us online at www.sixthsunfoundation.org.